THE BATTLE OF BALL'S BLUFF

THE BATTLE OF BALL'S BLUFF

All the Drowned Soldiers

BILL HOWARD

THE History PRESS

Published by The History Press
Charleston, SC
www.historypress.com

First published 2018

Manufactured in the United States

ISBN 9781467140737

Library of Congress Control Number: 2018945788

Contents

Acknowledgements

Each published work of history evolves as part of a continuum. Historians and authors who work to interpret the past are the beneficiaries of a rich legacy—a foundation of work laid by scores of others who passed this way before and made their best efforts to tell the story of the past. This book is no different. There are many whose work has helped to fill out the story of the Ball's Bluff battle and have added to my understanding of this "small battle with a long shadow." Special acknowledgement is extended to historians Kim Holien, Byron Farwell and James A. Morgan III for their great work in uncovering and explaining the details of Ball's Bluff. In the case of James Morgan, he has not only published historical accounts of the battle but has helped to better interpret and preserve the battlefield through land acquisition, signage and tours. There is no greater gift to military history than the preservation of the land hallowed by sacrifice. In this volume I have tried to provide an account that adds to the understanding of Ball's Bluff that is both historically accurate and readable. Military history has a tendency to become mired in the complex details of troop movements, which, while important, sometimes overwhelm the human dimension of war. I have tried to distill official military reports and primary source accounts into a volume that will be both informative and interesting to readers of all levels. The study of history is not the reserve of professional historians; the story of a nation's past belongs to its people. This book is intended to tell the story of Ball's Bluff in a way that will satisfy general readers and perhaps inspire some to pursue deeper study.

I came of age at a time in the years following the Civil War centennial commemoration of the early 1960s when scores of Civil War books were being published and old classics reprinted. I was fortunate to have had personal contact with many of the great historians and authors of those years, who inspired and cultivated my interest in both writing and history. I owe a lasting debt to Bruce Catton, Clifford Dowdey and, more recently, to Stephen B. Oates and Michael C.C. Adams. These authors were masters of combining solid history with great writing. I remain humbled by their support in my long-ago youth.

An earlier version of this book was published by H.E. Howard as part of his award-winning Virginia Civil War Battles and Leaders series in 1994. I am grateful to Harold Howard for his early support for my work and am pleased that I have been given the opportunity to significantly revise and expand this book some twenty-four years later.

In addition, I would like to extend thanks to so many whose support for my interest in history has been so important to me and to this book over the course of many years. Appreciation is extended to Michael Aikey, John Hennessy, Roger Hunt, Henry Deeks, Tom Broadfoot, Jeff McArdle and the late John Divine. I also owe thanks to so many others who have located and shared prints, maps, letters, books, photographs and other items associated with Ball's Bluff.

Ron Coddington of *Military Images* magazine was a lifesaver who came along at just the right time. Not only does he edit one of the most respected Civil War publications, but he also helped make this work so much better by sharing his digital scans of the Ball's Bluff images from the Ken Fleming Collection. His generosity in the interest of history saved a great deal of time and expense, and for that I will always be grateful.

The nonprofit Civil War Trust and the Friends of Ball's Bluff (FoBB) are incredible organizations that have taken Civil War preservation to an entirely new level. The work of these two organizations has helped to preserve significant portions of the Ball's Bluff battlefield. I have been a longtime contributing member of the trust and recently joined the FoBB. Sincere thanks to Tanya Roberts of the Civil War Trust and to the FoBB for supporting this project. I am pleased to report that a portion of the proceeds of this volume will be donated to support the important preservation work of these two fine organizations.

The U.S. Army Center of Military History granted permission to use the fine maps of Ball's Bluff developed for its 2001 published Staff Ride volume *Battle of Ball's Bluff*, by Ted Ballard. Special thanks to the center's Bryan J. Hockensmith.

The Massachusetts Historical Society granted permission to quote from the remarkable letter from Lieutenant Caspar Crowinshield to his mother, written the day after the Ball's Bluff battle, in its collection. Much appreciation is extended to Sabina Beauchard, who provided great assistance in navigating through the MHS collection.

Thanks also to James D. Julia Auctioneers of Fairfield, Maine, for the use of the photograph of the sword belonging to Major Paul Revere and to Laura E. Christiansen of the Thomas Balch Library in Leesburg, Virginia, for access to the library's Ball's Bluff Collection.

In addition, I would like to acknowledge Steve Meadow of Midland, Michigan, who graciously allowed for the use of some prized portrait images from his private collection. Appreciation is also extended to Ken Fleming, whose impressive collection of images of the men who fought at Ball's Bluff has added so much to this work. Collectors come in all sorts, but these dedicated guardians of the past have shared their collections in the interest of telling the human side of the Ball's Bluff story. This work is better for their contributions.

Appreciation is also extended to Mike Woodcock and Rob Balander for their assistance with many things digital, as well as to Dick Stanley, whose website, www.13thMississippi.com, offered a treasure-trove of valuable information about the Mississippians who fought at Ball's Bluff.

I am thankful to Paulette E. Morgan and my daughter, Katie Howard, who have shared and supported so much of my life journey through the past.

I also wish to thank my parents, William G. and Laura Howard, who long ago agreed to the quiet understanding that the route of all family vacations (no matter the end point) passed through Gettysburg.

Jane Balander has helped in so many ways in supporting the publication of this book. I value her great friendship and good work on my behalf. Quite simply, this book would not have come together without her assistance.

Lastly, I would like to express thanks to Kate Jenkins, Abigail Fleming and all of the good people at The History Press for their outstanding work on this volume and in helping to preserve the American past.

Introduction

Following the Southern victory at the First Battle of Manassas on July 21, 1861, a lull settled over the rolling fields of Northern Virginia. Although the armies of both North and South had eagerly anticipated the opportunity to prove their mettle on the battlefield, the ferocity of the Manassas contest came as a surprise. The realities of the battlefield consumed the heroic dreams of the young volunteers of the two opposing armies and destroyed the notion that the war would be a quick and bloodless affair. The Manassas experience was a jarring military education for the raw troops and provided a stark counter to the stirring imagery that had originally inspired them to march off to war. The effect was no less dramatic on the civilian population. Whereas in the months preceding Manassas there was an almost universal call to arms, Manassas provided an example for both sides to contemplate the broader implications of the struggle that had been joined. Manassas had been a confused fight, and while the inexperienced officers and men who maneuvered across the bloodied landscape were perhaps the first to realize it, the battle reinforced how ill-prepared for war the Union and Confederate armies were.

In a paper delivered before the Military Historical Society of Massachusetts in 1913, Lieutenant Charles Peirson, who had served as the adjutant of the Twentieth Massachusetts Infantry, remembered this period in the evolution of the Union volunteers of 1861:

> *The men of the Regiment, like all of the troops in the East at that time, were untrained by battle, never having heard the sound of a hostile bullet, and were*

of no more value as soldiers than were the Militia Regiments. Soldiers are not soldiers until they have been long enough together to have acquaintance with and respect for their officers, and have learned obedience with a belief in discipline, with a willingness to abide by it. The earlier Battle of Bull Run, which became a rout for want of discipline, proved nothing and taught nothing except the after-thought of the necessity for discipline.[1]

In the weeks following the first Manassas engagement, and largely because of the inexperience of the two opposing armies, neither General Joseph E. Johnston, commanding the Confederate forces, nor Major General George B. McClellan, now leading the Union army, was inclined to commit his army to another major battle in the few months that remained before winter.

President Abraham Lincoln gave McClellan command of the Military Division of the Potomac to bring order to the chaos inflicted by the Manassas defeat. President Lincoln was confident in his new commander, and McClellan sought to fully play out his role as the "Savior of the Union." It was a role that the Northern public desperately wanted to embrace. The author James Russell Lowell sarcastically wrote at the time, "There is nothing more touching than the sight of a nation in search of its great man, nothing more beautiful than its readiness to accept a hero on trust." No commander, he wrote, "ever had more…paid-up capital of fortune, this fame in advance, this success before succeeding, than General McClellan."[2]

Major General George B. McClellan. *Author's collection.*

McClellan was shaken by the condition of the army he inherited. He called it "a perfect pandemonium" and observed that there was "no army to command; a mere collection of regiments cowering on the banks of the Potomac, some perfectly raw, others dispirited by the recent defeat."[3]

While McClellan was busily engaged in training and reorganizing his newly named Army of the Potomac, the Confederate general Johnston believed that his force was too small to initiate an offensive and take advantage of the confusion following the Manassas battle. Compounding the

Confederate Quaker guns before Centreville, Virginia. *Library of Congress.*

command and administrative problems being faced by both commanders were the thousands of new troops that were daily being sent into the field. As a result of these factors, there was no significant military action along the Potomac River line separating the Union and Confederate armies for much of the three months that followed Manassas, save the sporadic firing that occasionally flared between nervous pickets posted at the key Potomac crossings.[4]

As autumn arrived in Virginia, Union and Confederate commanders continued their efforts to avoid another battle, while, at the same time, keeping a watchful eye on enemy movements. In furtherance of this purpose, Union and Confederate patrols often probed each other's lines in an attempt to estimate troop strength or discover some impending offensive. On both sides, the officers in charge of such operations were careful to see that such excursions did not escalate into serious confrontations. It was in such an environment, with General Johnston growing increasingly concerned about Union intentions along the Potomac line, that the ever-cautious general began recalling his troops from their more advanced and isolated positions in Northern Virginia toward a more concentrated defensive line. On September 27, 1861, Johnston's forces abandoned Munson's Hill, the Confederate army's closest outpost to Washington, D.C., and retired to Fairfax Court House, Virginia. In place of his Munson's Hill garrison, Johnston left behind so-called Quaker guns, logs cleverly carved and painted black to resemble cannons, which were then mounted on the earthworks to intimidate a pursuit by Union forces. On October 17, 1861, Johnston withdrew even farther beyond Fairfax Court House and began consolidating his forty-one thousand men along a more heavily fortified position known as the "Centreville line." This triangular line, with Centreville at the apex, stretched from Manassas Junction to the old Manassas battlefield, and offered an excellent defensive position for winter quarters.

Confederate major general Joseph E. Johnston. *Library of Congress.*

News of the Confederate movements interested General McClellan, and his army quickly moved to occupy the abandoned positions. This movement considerably strengthened the Union army's presence on the Confederate-held side of the Potomac. In reviewing his maps and dispatches, however, McClellan took note of one advanced Confederate position that had not been evacuated: Leesburg, Virginia, about thirty-five miles up the Potomac from Washington. Confederate infantry had occupied the town in early August 1861, and as a result of General Johnston's recent movements, the position of the Leesburg garrison was exposed, as it rested on the extreme left flank of the Confederate line.

Leesburg was strategically important to both armies for a number of reasons. More than ten fords or ferries provided access across the Potomac River and were within a few miles of the town to the east and north. On the Maryland side of these crossing points were the Chesapeake and Ohio Canal (C&O) and the Baltimore and Ohio Railroad. To the west of Leesburg were passes over the Catoctin Mountains offering openings to the fertile Loudoun Valley, and to the north were passes through the

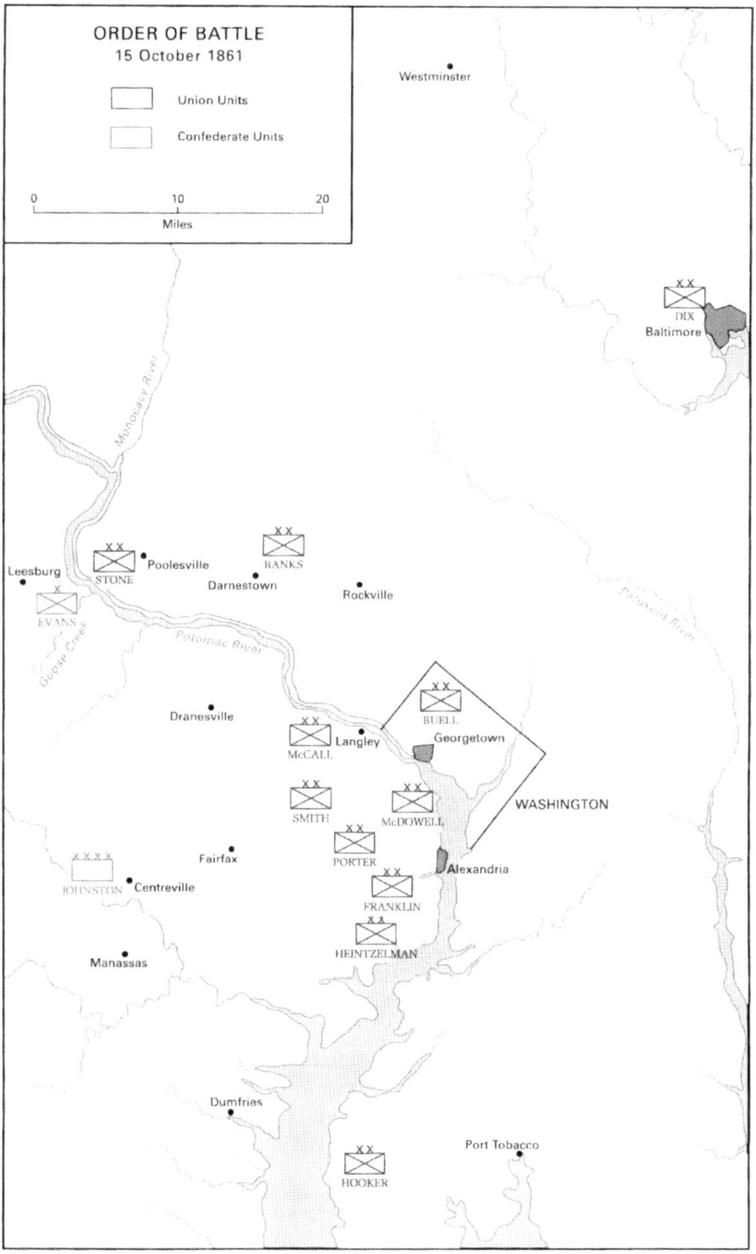

Situation in Northern Virginia, October 15, 1861. *Center for Military History.*

Blue Ridge Mountains. These gaps and passes, coupled with the impressive road network and fords, made Leesburg a central staging area for troop movements through Maryland and on to Washington, D.C.

Assuming that the small Confederate garrison force would abandon the town if pressured by Union troops (as the Confederates had abandoned other advanced positions when anticipating Federal advances), McClellan proposed that a small display of force near Leesburg might prompt the Confederates to evacuate the town without a fight. Such a bloodless victory with the result of securing Leesburg and a good portion of Northern Virginia for the Union would go a long way toward blunting the impact of the Manassas defeat and could reinvigorate morale both in the field and on the homefront as the war's first winter arrived.

1

Seizing Opportunity

At the time it appeared on General McClellan's topographical maps, Leesburg was a bustling town in rural Northern Virginia with a population of just over 1,600 resting thirty-five miles northwest of Washington. The town served as the seat of Loudoun County and was situated within a narrow band of rolling farmland bounded by the Catoctin Mountains to the west and the Potomac River to the east. About twenty-five miles upstream, where the Shenandoah River joins the Potomac, was Harpers Ferry, site of the Federal arsenal raided by the abolitionist John Brown in 1859.[5] Leesburg was garrisoned by a brigade of Confederate troops under the command of Colonel Nathan "Shanks" Evans. Evans had gained his nickname while at West Point. He attended the academy in the company of many young men who would go on to fight in the Civil War and was acquainted with many of the cadets and instructors who shared his time at the academy, including fellow Confederates Thomas J. "Stonewall" Jackson and Ambrose P. Hill and future Union generals George B. McClellan and Charles P. Stone. A native of South Carolina, Evans graduated with the class of 1848, ranking thirty-sixth out of thirty-eight graduates.[6] He had resigned his commission as a major in the Second U.S. Cavalry five months prior to the First Battle of Manassas. In physical appearance, Colonel Evans was well suited to his nickname. Following the Battle of Ball's Bluff, a Union officer captured in the fight who was introduced to the colonel described Evans as of "tall, brawny frame and unusual length of limb." This same officer added that the colonel's manners were "courteous and dignified."[7] Evans was regarded as a hero of First Manassas whose tactical skill and personal bravery during the battle helped turn the tide toward Confederate victory.

After Manassas, Evans was engaged in a lengthy correspondence with various Confederate officials regarding the status of his rank and his desire to be promoted to brigadier general. Evans had not received formal notice of his promotion to colonel until five days after the Manassas fight. In Richmond, Confederate inspector general Samuel Cooper advised General P.G.T. Beauregard that Evans had temporarily been assigned the rank of colonel, but if any "emergency arose," he could be assigned a higher rank. Evans had written to Confederate general Robert E. Lee (his old commander before the war) requesting his assistance in securing a brigadier general's star, but Lee had been unsuccessful, writing back two weeks later that "he could not make the arrangements [Evans] desired…[but] it will only be postponed a little while I hope. You are now a Colonel, [and] can command your brigade & will soon give cause I know for the advancement of the other step."[8]

Uncertain and anxious about his status and bristling at the thought of other officers with whom he had served in the prewar army receiving general's commissions in the Confederate forces, Evans also was shaken by personal tragedy while garrisoned at Leesburg. In September 1861, he learned that his mother had been killed in a bizarre accident back at the family plantation in Marion, South Carolina. She had been supervising the work of a slave who was repairing a roof on the main house when she was struck by a timber that had been discarded during the repairs. She survived a severe head trauma only a few hours. Colonel Evans was devastated when he received word of her passing, but the military situation in Northern Virginia required that he remain at his post.[9]

Confederate general P.G.T. Beauregard. *Author's collection.*

The 2,800 troops under Evans's overall command consisted of the Thirteenth, Seventeenth and Eighteenth Mississippi Infantry and the Eighth Virginia Infantry (supplemented variously by three or four companies of Virginia cavalry and the five guns of the First Company, Richmond Howitzers). These units formed the Seventh Brigade in General P.G.T. Beauregard's

I Corps of the Confederate Army of the Potomac and brought together a remarkable collection of personalities. The Eighth Virginia was led by a Southern gentleman lawyer–turned military officer, Eppa Hunton.[10] The thirty-nine-year old Hunton had served as a delegate to the Virginia Secession Convention and had been extremely vocal in denouncing the political wavering that preceded the signing of the Ordinance of Secession. As Virginia prepared for war, Hunton resigned his commission as a brigadier general in the state militia in order to accept field command. He was proud to have been appointed colonel of the Eighth Virginia, a regiment composed entirely of volunteers from Northern Virginia. Hunton's genteel bearing was in sharp contrast to that of Colonel William Barksdale of the Thirteenth Mississippi. Barksdale had attended the University of Nashville and studied law before the war but never forget his pioneer roots. He fought with the regular army during the Mexican War as both an enlisted man and as an officer and, from 1853 to 1861, served as a proslavery Democrat in the U.S. Congress. Barksdale returned to Mississippi when war erupted to seek a military appointment and was elected colonel of the Thirteenth Mississippi Infantry.[11] Both he and Hunton had participated in the Manassas battle, though distinction on the field had eluded them both.

The Seventeenth Mississippi also fought at Manassas, and its commanding officer, Colonel Winfield Scott Featherston, was a backcountry lawyer who had served with Barksdale (as well as Abraham Lincoln and Edward D. Baker) in Congress. Featherston's qualifications for military command primarily consisted of his political import, the respect of his men and his brief service as a volunteer in the war against the Creek Indians in 1836. Together with the physician-turned-colonel Erasmus R. Burt, who commanded the Eighteenth Mississippi Infantry, and Lieutenant Colonel Walter H. Jenifer, who led the three mixed companies of Virginia cavalry, these were the men who formed the officer corps of the Confederate forces at Leesburg.

The Mississippi troops that served in Evans's command were some of the finest troops serving in the Confederate army. Rough-hewn and toughened by agricultural life, they were natural marksmen who had grown up hunting the canebrakes and swamps of their native state. They were no-nonsense men who had already transformed into reliable soldiers, thereby adding great stability to Evans's command.

Evans's brigade served as an outpost on the extreme Confederate left flank. Its purpose was to observe the Potomac line, keeping an eye on the various fords and ferry crossings, as well as on the turnpike that linked Leesburg with Alexandria. A few miles to the east, on the north side of the Alexandria-

Winchester Turnpike, was a trapezoidal defensive work the Confederates constructed and named Fort Evans in honor of their commander. The earthen fort enclosed one and a half acres and was situated on high ground that offered a commanding view of the surrounding area and approaches.[12] Colonel Evans established his headquarters here and used the fort as a base from which to mount picket patrols and scouting missions. Fort Evans was the larger of two earthen defensive structures built by the Confederates. The other structure was a so-called masked battery that was built during August and September 1861. This simple trench-like artillery emplacement was located where the Edward's Ferry Road crossed Cattail Run and seems to have captivated the Union commanders. It was dug on the western bluff of the creek, rising about twenty feet above the bottomland. The fortification straddled the Edward's Ferry Road with a single parapet a deep ditch dug in front.[13] It was manned by a section of the Richmond Howitzers and likely featured a six-pounder field piece and a twelve-pounder howitzer. The artillery placed here commanded the road from Edward's Ferry into Leesburg.

The Confederate soldiers stationed in Leesburg seemed to enjoy their duties in and around the town and, as evidenced by surviving accounts, apparently experienced little trepidation about their exposed position. Long after the war, the Yale-educated Robert Stiles of the Richmond Howitzers remembered: "If ever soldiers had a more ideal time than we enjoyed at Leesburg, then I cannot conceive when or where it was. During the war, in hunger and thirst, in want and weariness and blood, our thoughts would often turn fondly back to our bucolic Loudoun paradise."[14]

Opposite Leesburg on the Maryland shore of the Potomac was a Union force numbering about ten thousand commanded by Brigadier General Charles Pomeroy Stone. Stone was an 1845 graduate of West Point and a respected officer. He had performed admirably in the early months of the war in establishing and securing the defenses of Washington and in ensuring President Lincoln's safety during the inauguration ceremonies in March 1861. His reward for this important service was the Maryland command, headquartered at Poolesville, which he referred to with a somewhat European flourish as the "Corps of Observation."[15] His assigned duty, like that of his Confederate counterpart Colonel Evans, was to observe the Potomac River line in the area between Point of Rocks, ten miles north of Leesburg, to Edward's Ferry, an important crossing site on the Maryland shore that offered direct road access to Leesburg. North of Stone, with orders to picket the area between Point of Rocks and Harpers Ferry, was a regiment under the command of Colonel John W. Geary; to the south, guarding the shoreline between Edward's Ferry and Washington, was a Union division under Major General Nathaniel P. Banks. In addition to these forces, two Union divisions under Generals George A. McCall and William F. Smith were positioned across from Washington on the Virginia side of the river.

Brigadier General Charles P. Stone. *Author's collection.*

Stone's Corps of Observation consisted of three infantry brigades commanded by Brigadier General Willis Gorman, Brigadier General Frederick W. Lander and Colonel Edward D. Baker. General Gorman's brigade was composed of five infantry regiments: the 34th New York, 42nd New York (known as the Tammany Regiment), 2nd New York State Militia, 1st Minnesota and 15th Massachusetts. General Lander's brigade consisted of the 7th Michigan, the 19th and 20th Massachusetts and Andrew's Company of Massachusetts Sharpshooters. The brigade under the command of Colonel Baker consisted of the 1st, 2nd, 3rd and 4th California Regiments. (These units were principally recruited in Pennsylvania but bore the designation of the western state in deference to Colonel Baker, who had been prominent in California politics before the war.) The California regiments were later re-designated as the Philadelphia Brigade and renumbered the 71st, 69th, 72nd and 106th Pennsylvania.[16] Also included in Stone's command were Kirby's Battery I, 1st U.S. Artillery; Vaughn's Battery B, 1st Rhode Island Light Artillery; Bunting's 6th New York State Militia Independent Battery; six companies of the 3rd New York Cavalry (known as Van Alen's Cavalry); and a detachment of Maryland cavalry known as the Putnam Rangers.

Colonel James H. Van Alen of the Third New York Cavalry. *Author's collection.*

Corporal Sidney S. Goodridge, Company K, Twentieth Massachusetts, at Camp Benton near Edward's Ferry. *Library of Congress.*

Like the Confederate forces garrisoned at Leesburg, the Union soldiers enjoyed their duties along the Potomac. The Union troops picketed the towpath of the Chesapeake and Ohio Canal, which paralleled the river along the northern bank and, on occasion, engaged in friendly conversation and trade with Confederate pickets on the opposite shoreline.[17] Although officers tried to discourage such intercourse, Captain William F. Bartlett of the Twentieth Massachusetts reported that even General Stone appreciated the practicality of such contact, although Bartlett himself was rather skeptical of the result. In a letter dated September 15, 1861, Bartlett wrote:

> *The Colonel* [William Raymond Lee] *was down at the river today with General Stone, and got one of our pickets to make advances to his neighbor opposite and draw him into a conversation across the river. They kept in the background, and listened to the dialougue* [sic], *which of course wasn't in a whisper. The rebel said they had but two or three hundred cavalry there, and only one or two batteries. Of course their information goes for what it is worth. But it seems rather laughable, the whole thing.*[18]

And so the armies waited, warily poised and casually observing each other from time to time, along the banks of the Potomac. Few in the ranks anticipated that the next few months would bring events of any great importance; most seemed content to enjoy the pleasures of town and country, believing that a new offensive was probably not likely to begin until the following spring.

2

"A Slight Demonstration"

While his soldiers were biding their time on the banks of the Potomac, General McClellan was growing increasingly concerned about the stability of the Union position between Point of Rocks and Washington. In the months after Manassas and his taking command of the Union forces, McClellan became convinced that his army was vastly outnumbered by the Confederates. Relying on spurious intelligence reports that inflated enemy strength, McClellan sent a series of rushed and paranoid-infused letters to General-in-Chief Winfield Scott back in Washington, D.C. McClellan not only insisted that his force was outnumbered but also believed that the Confederates were planning an imminent attack on the capital city. Scott sought to ease his rattled general and expressed confidence in the city's defenses, but McClellan would have none of it. He insisted that the Confederate army now numbered 150,000 against his paltry 55,000 and demanded more resources. On August 8, 1861, McClellan poured out his fears to his wife: "I have hardly slept one moment for the last three nights' knowing well that the enemy intend some movement & fully recognizing our own weakness. If Beauregard does not attack tonight I shall look upon it as a dispensation of Providence—he ought to do it."[19]

Ten days after composing this letter, and after General Stone had established his headquarters at Poolesville, Maryland, McClellan telegraphed his continued fears to Stone: "General Banks today confirms the belief that the enemy intends crossing the Potomac in your vicinity and moving on Baltimore or Washington." Stone, who disagreed with this evaluation, responded that only two Mississippi regiments were at Leesburg but suggested that if McClellan still thought an offensive was imminent, additional troops should be sent to his front. Still believing that a Confederate offensive was in the works, McClellan sent Stone reinforcements and informed the War Department that he expected a Confederate move on either Baltimore or Washington to be initiated along Stone's line.[20] Fearing superior Confederate numbers, McClellan was reluctant to precipitate a battle. Considering the public outcry following the debacle at Manassas, McClellan did not want to commit his forces until he held great numerical and tactical advantage, because, as he wrote Secretary of War Simon Cameron, he believed that "the fate of the nation and the success of the cause in which we are engaged [would] be mainly decided by the issue of the next battle to be fought by the army under my command."[21]

The Confederates also feared action in Northern Virginia. In late September, General Beauregard had written to Colonel Evans, warning: "The enemy is threatening our front," and advising Evans to "be prepared for any offensive movement against [him]." Beauregard directed Evans to delay the enemy march as long as practicable, making sure that he was not cut off from an effective line of retreat. Beauregard also noted that, given the current state of affairs, "we can at present send you no reinforcements."[22]

Although the situation in Northern Virginia was tense, General Beauregard was considering removing the Mississippi regiments from Evans's brigade to support another command. There was a question about Colonel Evans remaining at Leesburg. In the same letter in which Beauregard discussed the possible transfer of the Mississippi troops, he also proposed that if Evans were granted promotion to brigadier general, he would likely be given command of a new brigade at a different place. Because neither the promotion nor the reorganization of the brigade had taken place by early October, Evans and his men remained lodged around Leesburg, with Evans still believing that the Union army might attempt some flanking movement near his force.[23]

It was now mid-October, and the Confederates had still not attempted any Potomac crossing, but Evans's brigade at Leesburg continued to interest both McClellan and Stone. On October 13, Stone telegraphed McClellan that he "anticipated an early attempt by the enemy to secure Mason's or Harrison's Island, perhaps both, but probably the latter." A few days later, however, Stone reported the surprising news that the Confederate pickets had been withdrawn from their posts along the Potomac. On October 19, Stone provided McClellan with additional information about the withdrawal, which he had obtained from "an intelligent mulatto teamster, who had

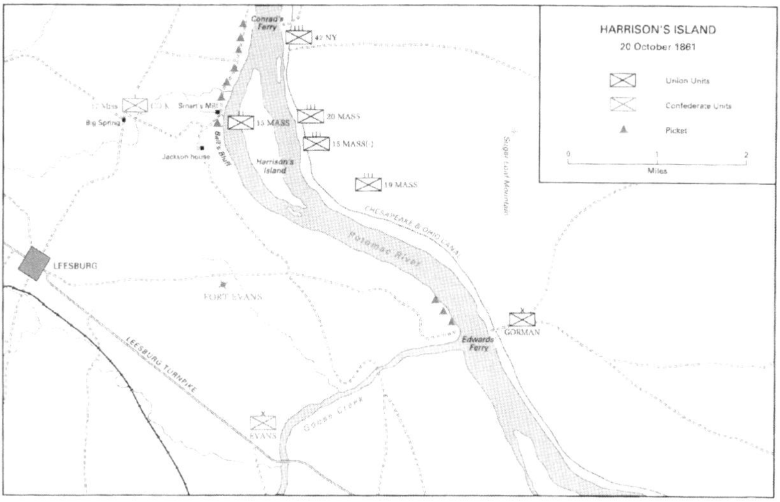

Positions along the Potomac River, October 20, 1861. *Center for Military History.*

deserted from the Thirteenth Mississippi Regiment, near Leesburg."[24] In this report, Stone indicated that, according to the teamster, the Confederates at Leesburg (Evan's brigade), concerned about the growing presence of Union troops on the Virginia side of the Potomac, were preparing to abandon the town. Stone indicated that he believed the reports to be true and that he had prepared "slight intrenchments [*sic*] on Harrison's Island," from which he believed a Union offensive could be launched.[25]

The Confederate movement, however, had been inspired not by a plan to attack Washington, D.C., but rather in response to the actions of another large Union force, under the command of General George A. McCall. McCall, a sixty-year-old officer who had graduated from West Point in 1822 and longed to be retired, commanded a division composed entirely of Pennsylvanians. McCall's twelve thousand men had crossed into Virginia and set up camp just outside Washington, D.C., near the town of Langley on October 9. The men had christened the encampment "Camp Pierpont" and hoped to spend a quiet winter there. It was this move by McCall's division, along with a brief exchange between pickets that took place around midnight on October 16 near Harpers Ferry, that inspired Colonel Evans to realign his defensive position.[26]

After learning of the scuffle between pickets, Colonel Evans interpreted the action as being preliminary to the long-anticipated flanking attack by

Union forces. Concerned that his small force was in jeopardy, Evans began pulling his scattered troops back from their positions around Leesburg. He concentrated his forces about eight miles to the south and set up a new line at Carter's Mill (near the Oatlands Plantation).[27] Evans accomplished the move without securing specific orders from his superior, General P.G.T. Beauregard. When an annoyed General Beauregard received word of the move, he directed his aide, Assistant Adjutant General Thomas Jordan, to send a message to Evans on October 17 requesting justification for the movement. The message read:

> *Your note of this day has been laid before the general, who wishes to be informed of the reasons that influenced you to take up your present position, as you omit to inform him. The point you occupy is understood to be very strong, and the General hopes you will be able to maintain it against odds should the enemy press across the river and move in this direction. To prevent such a movement and junction of Banks' forces with McClellan's is of utmost military importance, and you will be expected to make a desperate stand, falling back only in the face of an overwhelming enemy. In case, unfortunately you should be obliged to retire, march on this point and effect a juncture with* [t]*his corps.*
>
> *If you still deem it best to remain at Carter's Mill, the General desires you to maintain possession of Leesburg as an outpost by a regiment without baggage or tents, and to be relieved every three or four days.*[28]

In response to Beauregard's missive, Evans began moving his men back toward Leesburg on the night of October 19. These troop movements were observed by Union agents who were in the town and reported to McClellan's headquarters.[29]

While McClellan still did not wish to bring on a general engagement, he considered whether if the Confederates were so willing to abandon Leesburg as a result of a subtle move by Union forces, a small-scale advance along the line might produce even more significant results. McClellan believed this could all be accomplished with very little risk. It was a gamble he was willing to try, and on October 19, he ordered General McCall to march his division from its camp at Langley on the Virginia side of the Potomac along the Georgetown Turnpike toward Dranesville, Virginia (about twelve miles southeast of Leesburg). Once McCall completed this march, he was expected to return to Langley the following day. McCall's movement was accomplished with little difficulty but was based on the faulty

Union general George A. McCall.
Author's collection.

information that the Confederates were abandoning Leesburg, rather than returning to defend it. By the morning of October 20, Evans had entrenched his men along Goose Creek east of town and blocked the main road. The Confederate movements were observed by the Union signal station on Sugarloaf Mountain, which promptly alerted General McClellan by telegraph.[30] In reaction to this intelligence, McClellan sent orders to General Stone that same morning, advising him that McCall's division had occupied Dranesville and was in the process of sending out reconnaissance forces. Stone was instructed to "keep a good look out upon Leesburg to see if this movement has the effect to drive [the enemy] away." In closing, McClellan suggested that "perhaps a slight demonstration on [Stone's] part would have the effect to move them."[31]

Even before these orders were received at Stone's headquarters, the Confederates had gained knowledge of Union intentions. Having captured one of General McCall's couriers, Colonel Evans knew of McCall's movement on the Georgetown Turnpike even before Stone was advised. In reaction to the information, he maintained his position on Goose Creek at a place known locally as the "burnt bridge" (the site of a wooden bridge that had been destroyed earlier in the summer where the Leesburg Turnpike crossed Goose Creek) and took a defensive position on the northwest bank. Here, about four miles from Leesburg, Evans awaited McCall's advance. While Evans did move to concentrate his forces, he had not, as Stone believed, withdrawn his pickets from their posts along the Potomac. A scattered force of Confederates continued to keep a watch on the main Potomac fords.

General Stone moved without delay to comply with McClellan's order. Understanding that McCall's division had occupied Dranesville and was now moving westward on the Leesburg and Alexandria Turnpike, Stone tried to hold the Confederate troops around Leesburg in check by feigning a movement across two Potomac crossing sites at both Edward's Ferry and three and a half miles upriver at Smart's Mill Ford.

Union brigadier general Willis Gorman. *Author's collection.*

Early in the afternoon of October 20, General Stone, accompanied by a portion of Gorman's brigade—the Seventh Michigan Infantry, two companies of cavalry and some artillery—rode to Edward's Ferry. He ordered the artillery to lob a few shells across the river from the Maryland shore in a noisy demonstration and sent a small force over to the Virginia side in three flatboats that had been taken from the C&O Canal. Two companies of the First Minnesota Infantry made the crossing, while the balance of Gorman's troops remained on the Maryland side in support. As the Minnesota troops made their crossing, the Confederates on the Virginia shoreline retreated from view and the Minnesota troops were recalled back to the Maryland side of the river.[32] Such was the nature of the "slight demonstration" that McClellan had ordered Stone to make, an operation that was consistent with McClellan's dispatch. In the years after the Battle of Ball's Bluff, there would be much confusion concerning Stone's awareness of the precise nature of General McCall's movement. Importantly, as Stone made his demonstration, McCall's force had already been withdrawn from Dranesville. General McClellan insisted that he had made Stone aware of this, but most of Stone's tactical decisions that followed seem influenced by a belief that McCall's troops were available to support him if necessary.[33]

General Stone summarized the action at Edward's Ferry:

> *I ordered General Gorman to display his forces in view of the enemy, which was done without inducing any movement on their part, and then ordered three flat-boats to be passed from the canal into the river, at the same time throwing shells and spherical-case shot into the beyond the wood where the enemy was concealed and into all cover from which fire could be opened on boats crossing the river, to produce an impression that a crossing was to be made.*[34]

The Confederates observed the Union movements, but Colonel Evans was not deceived. Evans's main force was only two miles away from Edward's Ferry and could rapidly be mobilized if a genuine threat materialized at the crossing. He continued watching and waiting for the approach of the expected advance elements of McCall's division. From his strong position at Goose Creek, Colonel Evans encouraged his men with a patriotic speech and prepared them for the possibility of a difficult fight against vastly superior numbers of enemy troops—without the promise of reinforcements.[35] Private Albert Wymer Henley of the Thirteenth Mississippi Infantry remembered: "On our way, we were met by [Colonel] Evans, who halted us and in a few words exhorted us to be valiant, heroic and brave, after which [Colonel Barksdale] proposed three cheers for the South and three more for [Colonel] Evans, both of which were cheerfully given. Then we right faced and proceeded on our way."[36]

General Stone was uncertain of the effect his demonstration had on the Confederates. In fact, he was not even sure that the Confederates were still at Leesburg. It was possible that Evans had abandoned the town and withdrawn all the way up Goose Creek toward the main Confederate army at Centreville. In order to gain better information about Confederate movements, Stone sent an order to Colonel Charles Devens, the Harvard-educated commander of the Fifteenth Massachusetts Infantry, requesting that a reconnaissance party be assembled to cross over into Virginia and scout inland toward Leesburg.[37] Devens, who was holding his men in reserve at Conrad's Ferry, was ordered to march several companies of his regiment downriver and take position on Harrison's Island opposite Ball's Bluff.[38] It was a complex operation for his inexperienced troops. The men would march along the Maryland shore, cross over to Harrison's Island in the middle of the Potomac and then cross the river again to make their scout into Virginia. Although Stone had wanted the patrol to leave as soon as the order was received, Colonel Devens could not

Colonel Charles Devens of the Fifteenth Massachusetts Infantry. *Collection of Ken Fleming.*

immediately be located (he was apparently at church), and it was not until about sunset that Captain Chase Philbrick, Lieutenant Church Howe and perhaps twenty volunteers from Company H, Fifteenth Massachusetts, started on their dangerous mission. Philbrick, a thirty-eight-year-old New Hampshire stonecutter prior to his enlistment, had been commissioned captain when the volunteer regiment was organized in May 1861.[39] He was selected for this mission, not because of any military background but because he had already scouted the area a few nights earlier, looking for signs of Confederate troops.

Captain Philbrick's orders were to cross the Potomac from Harrison's Island, the whale-shaped, two-mile-long, half-mile-wide island in the middle of the river, to the Virginia side at a spot known locally as Ball's Bluff.[40] The site could be intimidating to a Union scouting party operating in darkness, with its rugged terrain, muddy riverbank and precarious wood-tangled cliffs that rose sixty to one hundred feet from the shoreline. The area presented such a tremendous challenge to attacking troops that the Confederates had left it largely unguarded. General Stone knew it was undefended because he had been sending scouting patrols across the river to the bluff for several weeks without incident. These patrols had discovered an old worn cart path about ten or twelve feet in width in the woods along the shoreline that led up the bluff to a ridge overlooking Leesburg and the town's primary north–south road. It was this ridgeline that was the object of Captain Philbrick's mission. Specifically, Stone's orders to Philbrick were to "cross from the island and explore by a path through the woods, little used, in the direction of Leesburg, to see if he could find anything concerning the enemy's position in that direction."[41]

Captain Chase Philbrick of the Fifteenth Massachusetts Infantry. *Author's collection.*

It took several hours for Philbrick's party to reach the Virginia shore in two skiffs. By the time the men found their way to the top of Ball's Bluff, the moon was full in the sky and a foggy mist had risen from the river, filling the rolling valley that stretched away from the bluff toward Leesburg. The party found the cart path with little difficulty and had advanced about one mile, when,

Harper's Weekly depiction of Captain Philbrick's scout, published October 26, 1861. *Author's collection.*

upon reaching the ridgeline, Captain Philbrick saw in the distance what he judged to be an assembly of fifteen to twenty tents. He later claimed that he had approached to within 130 yards of the tents and observed neither campfires nor picket guards. Flush with this information, Philbrick and his patrol quickly backtracked, reaching Harrison's Island at about 10:00 p.m.[42] Philbrick reported to Colonel Devens and was then ordered to locate General Stone at Edward's Ferry to provide him with the details of the reconnaissance.

Despite the delay, the report submitted by Captain Philbrick at about 11:00 p.m. was warmly received by General Stone, who immediately recognized what he later referred to as "a very nice little military chance" in the existence of the unguarded Confederate camp. Stone entertained no doubts regarding the accuracy of Philbrick's report. "It seemed to me," Stone later recalled, "precisely one of those pieces of carelessness on the part of the enemy that ought to be taken advantage of."[43] Stone did not have the authority to order a general advance, but he could order small scouting or raiding parties to explore his front. Seizing the perceived opportunity, Stone decided to send a small force consisting of four companies of the Fifteenth Massachusetts, under the command of Colonel Devens, across the Potomac to Ball's Bluff in order to capture or disperse the Confederate camp.[44]

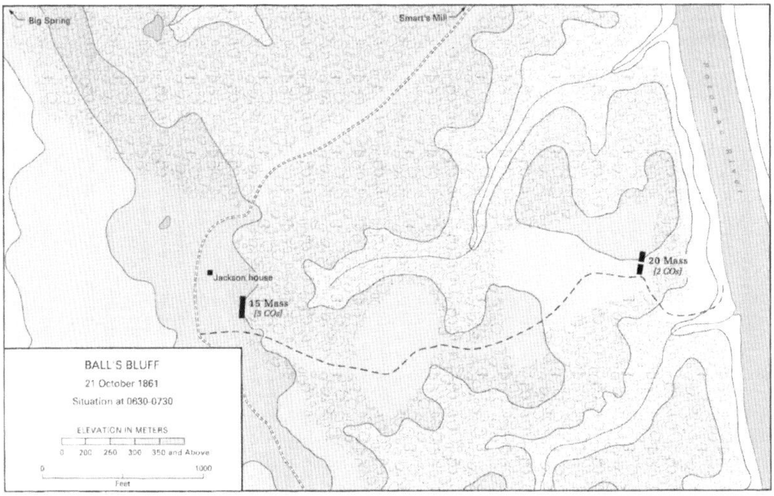

Initial positions of the Fifteenth and Twentieth Massachusetts Infantry Regiments on the morning of October 21, 1861. *Center for Military History.*

Colonel Charles Devens and staff after Ball's Bluff. *Library of Congress.*

Colonel William R. Lee of the Twentieth Massachusetts Infantry. *Author's collection.*

Colonel Devens's force of about three hundred men was to be supported by Colonel W. Raymond Lee and about one hundred men of the Twentieth Massachusetts, who would also cross the Potomac and wait for Devens in a defensive position at the top of the bluff. In order support these troops, two twelve-pounder mountain howitzer cannons from Lieutenant Frank French's Battery I, First U.S. Artillery, were positioned on the C&O towpath opposite Harrison's Island to deal with any action that might develop atop Ball's Bluff. Additional artillery support was provided by four twelve-pounder rifled guns from Battery B, First Rhode Island Light Artillery that were positioned on the towpath near the island. These guns were under the overall command of Colonel Lee. The two remaining guns of the Rhode Island Battery remained north of Conrad's Ferry to protect that ford. Stone also ordered the First California Infantry and the Forty-Second New York to provide support, if needed, from their reserve positions at Conrad's Ferry.[45]

Lieutenant Henry Livermore Abbott of the Twentieth Massachusetts was struck by the contrasting moods of the two primary field commanders, Colonels Devens and Lee, as the operation unfolded. He wrote that Devens "seemed like a man who had made up his mind that he was going on a forlorn hope," while Lee "was in the merriest of moods," cracking jokes and quoting inspirational lines from the classics.[46] The moods likely reflected the distinct nature of the assigned missions, as Devens would be advancing inland and feeling toward the enemy while Lee would be serving in reserve as defensive support. It may all have been hindsight, of course, but Lieutenant Abbott maintained that Colonel Lee kept pressing various tactical contingencies and questioning Devens on what he might do in response. This, recalled Abbott, seemed to irritate Devens. According to Abbott, Lee understood the inherent weakness of the Union position and noted that "in case of defeat, no retreat was possible. We must either conquer or die."[47]

Colonel Devens started out about midnight with five companies (not the four Stone had ordered) of his regiment but immediately encountered difficulties. The Potomac was swollen from recent rains, and the always

Lieutenant Henry Livermore Abbott, Twentieth Massachusetts Infantry. *Henry Deeks Collection.*

unpredictable current was now even more treacherous because of the increased flow. A Massachusetts officer who had been on the Harvard crew team recalled that the Potomac was moving so fast the only way to cross was to move diagonally from the landing point and let the current carry them to their intended destination.[48] Captain Thomas F. Winthrop of the Nineteenth Massachusetts Infantry made a similar observation, noting that "the river was full and its current swift by reason of recent rains." Captain Winthrop added that

> *on account of the strong current it was impossible to make a direct crossing. It became necessary to pole the boats up along the Maryland side, out of the current, some five or six hundred yards, and then it was only by the exhausting labor that they could be brought to the proper landing on the island. The poles used for propelling the boats were cut that morning from living trees, and on account of the depth and strength of the current were necessarily large and unwieldly* [sic].

Winthrop estimated that until a rope was obtained from a canalboat and was strung across the Potomac on the Maryland side of the channel to be used as a guide wire "no boat could make the passage to and from the island in less than an hour and a quarter."[49] Colonel Devens had only three small boats available with a total capacity of about thirty men to transport his forces from Harrison's Island to the Virginia shore. The regimental historian of the Nineteenth Massachusetts Infantry described the watercraft as "three miserable hulks, dignified by the name of scows."[50] Regardless of the insufficiency of transport, it was a cool, damp October night, and the men were ordered to forego cumbersome overcoats and knapsacks. Devens reasoned that the temperature would rise after daylight, and the men would be forced to discard the extra covering. It was not until about 4:00 a.m. that Devens's men reached the Virginia shoreline. The men were cold and tired but made it up the cart path to the top of Ball's Bluff.[51] Colonel Lee soon followed with the two companies of his Twentieth Massachusetts.

Harrison's Island had largely been cleared for farming, but what the Union soldiers found on the Virginia shore was a much different landscape and challenge. The historian of the Nineteenth Massachusetts recalled: "Into the scow, horses, men, and artillery piled, reached the Virginia shore, ascended the bank, ten feet high—clayey and slippery—and then climbed up the bluff, 100 to 150 feet high, by handfuls."[52] While the Potomac side of Ball's Bluff was a mix of scrub trees and boulders, the top of the bluff revealed an open grassy field of ten to twelve acres; the cart path from the river ran through the field and veered toward the left and into the woods beyond. Devens's detachment began its advance down this path at about 6:00 a.m. and had traveled about a mile when it reached a heavy rail fence on the far side of the woods. On the other side of this fence was another cleared field, which extended to the right up to the road that ran from Leesburg to Conrad's Ferry.[53] When Devens and his men advanced from this position to the ridge from which Philbrick had seen the Confederate camp the night before, they saw nothing but another slight ridge in the distance with a single row of trees on top. With no tents or enemy in sight, Colonel Devens turned to Captain Philbrick and asked, "Are we not mistaken?" It was soon clear that the Confederate camp did not exist, except perhaps in the mind of a nervous officer who had not fully investigated his apparent sighting. Immediately after Philbrick's mistake was realized, at about 7:00 a.m., Colonel Devens sent Lieutenant Church Howe back to General Stone at Edward's Ferry to report that the Confederate camp did not exist and that the party had discovered no sign of the enemy but he felt confident he could hold his position.[54]

Stone sent back word to Devens, instructing him to "use [the] opportunity to observe the approaches to Leesburg and the position and force of the enemy in the vicinity." If Devens found no signs of the enemy, he was ordered to take a position where he "could observe well and be secure until his party could be strengthened sufficiently to make a valuable reconnaissance…to ascertain the position and force of the enemy."[55]

While Devens's force was making its reconnaissance, Stone decided to feign another movement downriver at Edward's Ferry to divert Confederate attention away from Devens's men.[56] General Gorman was ordered to put a small force across the Potomac to be deployed as skirmishers while the Third New York Cavalry under Major John Mix scouted the area of Goose Creek in search of the enemy. Although Major Mix's troopers encountered a company of Mississippi infantry and engaged in a brief skirmish near the position of the masked Confederate battery on the Edward's Ferry Road, it suffered no losses and succeeded in capturing one prisoner. In reporting the action to McClellan, Stone referred to it as "a gallant reconnaissance."[57]

Upon receiving Lieutenant Howe's report regarding the nonexistent Confederate camp, Stone was still pleased that Devens had been able to advance within sight of Leesburg without being detected. Thinking that Devens might be able to maintain his position near Ball's Bluff long enough to conduct a more detailed scout, Stone requested that ten cavalrymen be sent to Devens in order to better observe his flanks and assist the force in communicating more efficiently with headquarters. Stone also ordered Lieutenant Colonel George H. Ward of the Fifteenth Massachusetts to take the five remaining companies of the regiment across the river and take possession of the stone grist building at Smart's Mill Ford on the Virginia side (about half a mile north of Ball's Bluff).[58] Most importantly, however, at about this time Stone placed Colonel Edward D. Baker in overall command of the reconnaissance mission.

Baker was probably a poor choice to command such an operation. While he had achieved much in civilian life as a politician and attorney, his military background was limited to some brief volunteer service rendered in the Black Hawk War and as the colonel of the Fourth Illinois Infantry during the Mexican War. Although his supporters would later wax eloquent on this aspect of Baker's very full and impressive life, the fifty-year-old Baker's primary qualification for military command was his political prominence and deep friendship with President Abraham Lincoln. Baker had once shared a law office with Lincoln in Springfield, served as a congressman from Illinois and was most recently serving as a U.S. senator from Oregon.[59] Baker had helped carry California and Oregon

Colonel Edward D. Baker. *Collection of Ken Fleming.*

for Lincoln in the 1860 election, and it was Baker who proudly introduced the president-elect during the long tour from Springfield to Washington as Lincoln traveled to the inauguration in February 1861. The two were so close that Lincoln named his second son Edward Baker Lincoln after his good friend. Not all who were close to the president were impressed by the senator-turned-military officer, however. Elizabeth Grimsley, a cousin to Mary Lincoln, attended a breakfast with the president and Baker on the morning of May 8, 1861, and commented: "I cannot bear that man. He seems to have such a supreme contempt for lesser intellects, that it quite lowers his own in my estimation."[60] Baker attended the breakfast with the president in order to solicit a major general's commission. He had already been offered a brigadier general's commission but was forced to decline it because of constitutional restrictions that prohibited a sitting member of Congress to hold active military rank above that of colonel. While all of that was being sorted, Baker accepted the rank of colonel in June. On September 21, 1861, Baker was tendered the appointment to the rank of major general, but he had made no formalized reply to the offer at the time of Ball's Bluff.

General Stone later wrote that he had a conversation with Baker prior to placing him in command at Ball's Bluff, informed him of McCall's advance on Dranesville and "detailed to him the means of transportation across the river…the sufficiency of which he was to be the judge." Stone

Patriotic envelope addressed and signed by Colonel Baker. *Author's collection.*

claimed that he also noted his intention to put more troops across the river at Edward's Ferry and told Baker that there were Confederate entrenchments and a masked battery between Ball's Bluff and Edward's Ferry that would prohibit any movement to the north. According to Stone, he then "left it to Baker's discretion, after viewing the ground, to retire the troops from the Virginia shore under the cover of his guns and the fire of the large infantry force, or to pass over re-enforcements in case he found it practicable and the position on the other side strong and favorable." Stone cautioned that while he was "extremely desirous of ascertaining the exact position and force of the enemy in our front" he "wished no advance unless the enemy were in inferior force." In addition to Baker's California Brigade, Stone assigned the Tammany Regiment (Forty-Second New York) and the Fifteenth and Twentieth Massachusetts to Baker's temporary command.[61]

Stone's order to Baker echoed the cautionary direction dictated to Stone by General McClellan. Back in August, when Stone was first given command of the Potomac Line, McClellan had instructed:

> *You will keep the main body of your force united in a strong position near Poolesville, and observe the dangerous fords with strong pickets that can dispute the passage until reinforced….Should you see the opportunity of capturing or dispersing any small parties by crossing the river, you are at liberty to do so, though great discretion is recommended in making such a movement. The general object of your command is to observe and dispute the passage of the river and the advance of the enemy….I leave your operations much to your own discretion, in which I have the fullest confidence.*[62]

When Stone gave command of the Virginia operation to Colonel Baker, he apparently believed that Baker would follow this same course of guidance. Summarized to its essential elements, Baker was to see whether a small display of Union force might cause the Confederates to abandon Leesburg and retire up Goose Creek toward the main Confederate army at Centreville. Baker was not to press the issue but merely test whether the Confederates would abandon the town in response to the Union feint. In accepting command, Baker requested that Stone put his orders in writing so that he might "have some written authority for assuming command." Stone hastily summarized the orders on a small slip of paper: "Colonel: In case of heavy firing in front of Harrison's Island, you will advance the California regiment of your brigade or retire the regiments under Colonels

Lee and Devens upon the Virginia side of the river, at your discretion, assuming command on arrival."[63] Colonel Baker took the slip of paper, read it, folded it and placed it, as was his custom, in the interior band of his hat. Whether Baker wanted his orders in writing because he wanted proof of his authority to assume command or because he did not completely understand Stone's intentions is uncertain. There is little question, however, that from the moment Baker left Stone's headquarters at about 9:30 a.m. on the morning of October 21, Baker was intent on bringing as many troops as possible over to the Virginia side of the Potomac and engaging whatever Confederates force he happened to find there.

Colonel Edward D. Baker. *Author's collection.*

3

The Battle Is Joined

Since mid-August, 1861, Company K of the Seventeenth Mississippi Infantry (the "Magnolia Guard") had patrolled the area of Ball's Bluff, observing the movements of the Union troops on the Maryland side of the Potomac without incident. On the morning of October 21, 1861, Company K and its commanding officer, Captain William R. Duff, were camped about two miles northeast of Leesburg at a spot known as Big Spring. This area was part of a large, one-thousand-acre farm owned by George Washington Ball, a nephew of the nation's first president. It was Ball who gave his name to the bluff overlooking the river. Although Colonel Devens believed that the Union river crossing had gone unobserved, Duff's Confederates had shadowed Devens's advance along the cart path.[64] While Devens advanced, about one hundred men of the Twentieth Massachusetts under Colonel W. Raymond Lee took position on the Bluff to serve in reserve.

Colonel Lee was a fifty-four-year-old businessman in his civilian life back in the Boston suburb of Roxbury, Massachusetts. A distant relative of Confederate general Robert E. Lee, he had attended, but not graduated, from West Point after beginning his studies there in 1825. While at West Point, he had befriended future Confederate president Jefferson Davis as well as others who went on to serve in the Confederate army. For reasons lost to history, Lee did not graduate with his class of 1829. Just days before graduation, Lee disappeared from the institution to return home in search of his father, who was suffering from a reported "brain attack." He was invited to return to West Point but never did, electing instead to pursue a

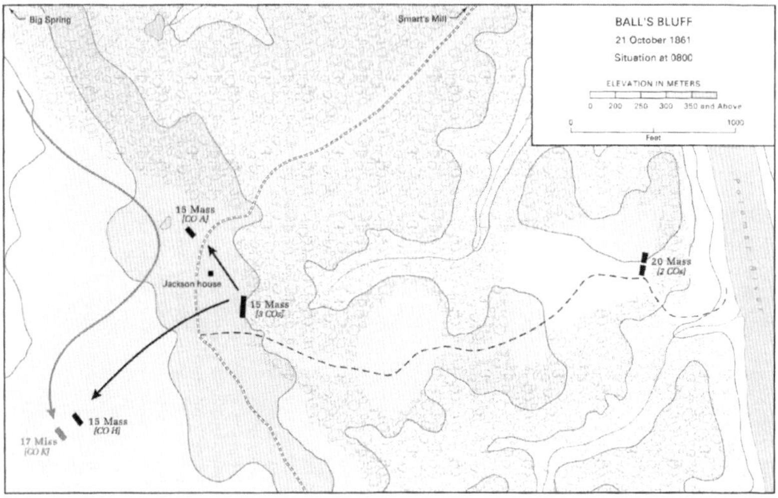

Skirmish near the Jackson House, morning of October 21, 1861. *Center for Military History.*

career in business and industry. He taught mathematics at Harvard, served as the general superintendent of the Boston and Providence Railroad and married Helen Maria Amory, the daughter of one of Boston's wealthiest merchants.[65] Lee was appointed colonel of the Twentieth Massachusetts Infantry in July 1861, and while he had not had much active service in the military over the course of his career, he considered himself an experienced military officer.[66] As Lee considered his position atop Ball's Bluff in a field surrounded by woods on all sides and the river to his rear, he was concerned that the enemy could launch an attack from the concealment of the tangled forest. He decided to deploy pickets to probe the area to the north and south of his position while he awaited Devens's return.

At about 7:00 a.m., one of these picket patrols, led by Adjutant Charles L. Peirson of the Twentieth Massachusetts, stumbled into Duff's Confederates while scouting around the right end of Lee's line. As the party approached a deep gully, Sergeant William R. Riddle and three men of Company I, Twentieth Massachusetts, pressed forward, peered over the edge of the depression and were greeted with gunfire from Duff's pickets. One bullet struck Sergeant Riddle in his right elbow, shattering the bone. Captain Bartlett of the Twentieth described the scene: "It was now about sunrise when we heard these three or four shots in rapid succession on our right. In a few minutes my first sergeant was brought in, shot through the elbow. He was fainting from loss of blood. We tied a handkerchief around his arm and sent him down to the river."[67]

Sergeant Riddle, a lithographer from New York City in private life, became the first casualty; the serious wound would later require amputation.[68]

Captain Duff was a competent officer, and as soon as he learned of the Union crossing and the exchange with his pickets he sent word to Colonel Evans, who was still holding the position at Goose Creek. Duff quickly began collecting all of the men that he could assemble and set off to confront Lee's pickets with about forty-five men. As he moved along the long ravine to the top of the ridge near the home of the widowed Margaret Jackson at about 8:00 a.m., his force was observed by some of Devens's men. Duff expected only a small force and was surprised by the large number of Union troops he encountered. What followed was a fifteen- or twenty-minute firefight in the open country beyond Philbrick's ridge, west of the Jackson House. Colonel Devens had about three hundred men in his command and ordered Captain Philbrick and the sixty-five men of Company H forward to drive the enemy off. This demonstration of strength was too much for Duff's small band of soldiers, and the Confederates retreated about three hundred yards down the slope of the hill in the direction of Leesburg and then halted. Captain Philbrick's company continued the advance, and in the confusion, Captain Duff's Mississippians apparently thought the Union troops were reinforcements arriving from Colonel Evans. Captain Duff called out to the advancing line and ordered the approaching force to halt. Duff made the plea repeatedly, and each time, the advancing soldiers replied, "We are friends." Just as Philbrick and his men advanced to within sixty yards of Duff's men, Duff realized that these were not Confederate troops coming to his support but rather the Union infantry he had just recently encountered. He immediately ordered his men to fire.[69]

The volley smashed into the Union line, knocking down several Massachusetts soldiers and sending the line staggering backward. A second volley inspired a fragmented withdrawal, but Philbrick was able to stabilize his line. Colonel Devens was about to order up Company G to come to Philbrick's support when he received reports of Confederate cavalry arriving on the field from Leesburg. Devens had had enough and broke off the engagement by pulling his troops back to the bluff, where he could get support from the Twentieth Massachusetts waiting there. The Union troops retired in good order with losses numbering one man killed, two missing and nine wounded. The Confederates suffered one man seriously wounded and two men slightly wounded. As Devens's line fell back, Captain Duff ordered his men to retire, fearing that the Union troops might work their way around the rear of his line and cut his force off from the road to Leesburg. Duff was pleased to see Colonel Jenifer's cavalry arriving, accompanied by four companies of Mississippi infantry (two from the Eighteenth Regiment, one from the Thirteenth and one from the Seventeenth). The Mississippians took position in some earthworks on Duff's right flank. Captain Lorenzo D. Fletcher, who commanded the lone company from the Thirteenth Mississippi, described the action near the Jackson House:

> *Upon my arrival there, I encountered the pickets of the enemy, who held a position along a line of fence. They opened a fire upon my company, which was returned, the pickets of the enemy falling back into the field and some of them occupying positions in and around the house of Mrs. Jackson. My company continued to advance until we reached the fence just left by the enemy who continued to fire upon us from the field and house, the fire being constantly returned by my men.*[70]

Inexplicably, however, after retiring to the bluff, Devens then regrouped his men and moved forward again, back to the position where he first encountered Duff's men. This was along a fence line near the edge of the woods south of the Jackson House. In making this advance, Devens may have been buoyed by the failure of the Confederates to pursue him, but as he moved forward, he made two command errors. He failed both to advise Colonel Lee of his tactical intentions and did not wait at the bluff to see if any additional orders were forthcoming from General Stone following Lieutenant Howe's briefing to the general about first contact with the enemy.

Thirty-three years after the events unfolded at Ball's Bluff, Charles H. Eager, formerly an officer in the Fifteenth Massachusetts, recalled the back-and-forth flow of the action. Eager wrote:

> *When Col. Devens with five companies of the regiment, reached the position of the "supposed camp," he had every reason to believe his presence was unknown to the enemy; and as his men were well concealed in the woods, he decided to remain for a while and see what information regarding the strength of the enemy could be obtained by daylight. After posting his videts he and Capt. Philbrick worked their way, under cover as much as possible, in the direction of Leesburg, but saw mothing of the enemy.*

About this time the videts discovered the enemy's picket on the road from Conrad's Ferry to Leesburg, which proved to be Capt. W.L. Duff, Co. K, 17th Miss., stationed at Big Spring, with pickets at different points in the vicinity. Capt. Duff had drawn in his pickets and was moving toward Leesburg, when Col. Devens ordered Co. H Capt. Philbrick to move forward and attack him, and Co. A, Capt. Lockwood, to move to the right and cut off his retreat to the river. Upon the appearance of Capt. Philbrick, Capt. Duff retreated through the cornfield some distance to a rifle-pit or ditch, where they opened fire on Co. H, which was returned with spirit, and a lively skirmish ensued for a few minutes. Co. H lost one man killed and nine wounded.

As Col. Devens was about to reinforce Capt. Philbrick, a body of the enemy's cavalry was reported on his left, and he ordered Capt. Philbrick to return to the woods. After waiting some time, and no enemy appearing, he decided to move back to the position of Col. Lee, with 100 men of the 20th Mass. on the bluff. After the woods had been thoroughly scouted, and no enemy found, Col. Devens again advanced to his former position through a line of skirmishers on the high ground by the Jackson House, his forces being stationed at different points in the woods.[71]

In his later testimony to Congress on the matter, Colonel Devens said:

We moved about for some-time, selecting various points of observation for the purpose of ascertaining what was to be seen, reconnoitering the country as thoroughly as we could, getting as good an idea of it as possible, in order to be able to answer any questions that might be asked me on my return. After this I returned to my regiment in the woods. At this time I deemed it my duty to report, as my force had not been discovered and I was in a good position and well protected.[72]

Colonel Devens expressed no great concern over the Confederates on his front. Earlier, when Lieutenant Howe reported to him at about 8:00 a.m., Devens had directed him to return at once to General Stone and report on the skirmish that had just taken place. Pursuant to the original orders General Stone had given to Devens for the patrol at Ball's Bluff, Devens maintained his position and ordered skirmishers to secure the brow of the hill in front of his line and on his right and left flanks. Lieutenant Howe had moved quickly to the rear following the same path Devens had taken from the bluff. As he emerged from the woods into

Left: James Bonney of Company C, Fifteenth Massachusetts Infantry; *Right*: Sergeant Frederick Sibley of Company B, Fifteenth Massachusetts Infantry. *Collection of Ken Fleming.*

the clearing at the top of the bluff he encountered Colonel Lee. Lee was anxious for a fight and told Howe to inform General Stone "that if he wants to open a campaign in Virginia, now is the time."[73]

But if Colonel Lee was embracing the prospects of battle, Lieutenant Howe, who had already scouted much of the front, was less confident and shared his concerns with just about every officer he encountered. Howe continued on his mission as instructed by Colonel Devens, but upon reaching Harrison's Island, he found Lieutenant Colonel George H. Ward and related a harrowing tale of impending disaster for the Union forces at Ball's Bluff. Ward had been ordered to take the remainder of the Fifteenth Massachusetts across the river and secure Smart's Mill Ford, but as he listened to Howe's account of the morning's skirmish, both he and Howe believed his proper place was to directly reinforce Devens. Devens was in a tenuous position, Howe warned, and was in need of Ward's support. Ward responded that although his orders were to secure Smart's Mill Ford, if Devens needed him,

Left: Samuel Fletcher of Company H, Fifteenth Massachusetts Infantry; *Right*: Lieutenant Leonard Wood of the Fifteenth Massachusetts Infantry. *Collection of Ken Fleming.*

he would move to support the other unit. Convinced by his conversation with Lieutenant Howe that this was the situation, Ward prepared to cross his men over to Ball's Bluff to come to Devens's assistance.

When Howe finally reached the Maryland shore, he met Colonel Baker on the C&O canal towpath at about 10:00 a.m. Howe described to Baker the situation at Ball's Bluff and succeeded in stirring Baker's martial blood. "I am going down immediately, with my whole force, to take command," Baker declared, as he spurred his horse toward the crossing site. After this series of chance meetings, in which Howe's description of the situation on Ball's Bluff seemed to grow increasingly desperate with each retelling, Howe arrived at General Stone's headquarters at Edward's Ferry. Howe told Stone about the skirmish, repeated Colonel Lee's optimistic message and informed him that rather than secure Smart's Mill Ford, Lieutenant Colonel Ward's detachment was now moving to support Devens at Ball's Bluff. Apparently under the impression that Colonel Baker had directed

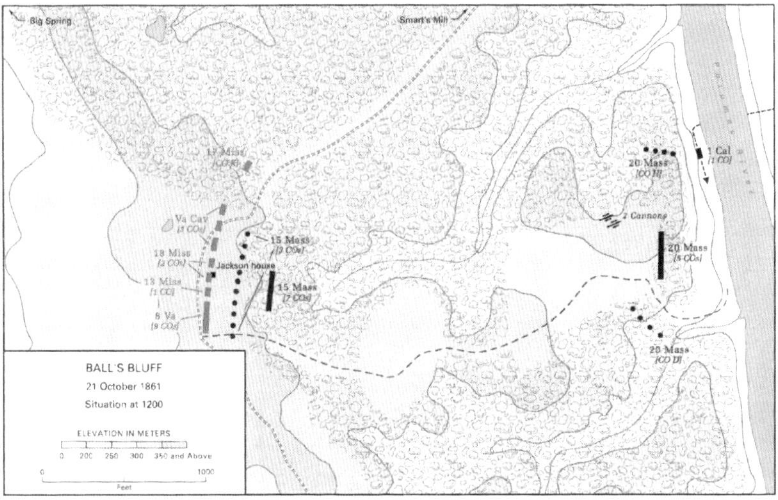

Battle action near the Jackson House, noon, October 21, 1861. *Center for Military History.*

this change in plans, Stone responded that "Colonel Baker is at that place [presumably Ball's Bluff] and will arrange these things to suit himself." Stone then dismissed Howe, instructing him to warn Baker to be careful of his right flank. Shortly after Howe left his headquarters, Stone sent a telegraph to McClellan: "The enemy has been engaged opposite Harrison's Island. Our men are behaving admirably."[74]

When McClellan received Stone's communication, it was the first he learned that the situation at Ball's Bluff was more than just a scouting operation. McClellan telegraphed McCall and ordered him to remain at Dranesville, only to discover that McCall had already withdrawn his force to Langley as directed in his original orders. McClellan ordered both McCall and General Nathaniel Banks to prepare for a move to support Stone if required. McClellan also sent a message to Stone, asking,

> *Is the force of the enemy now engaged with your troops opposite Harrison's Island large? If so, and you require more support than your division affords, call upon General Banks, who has been directed to respond. What force, in your opinion, would it require to take Leesburg? Answer at once, as I may require you to take it to-day: and if so, I will support you on the other side of the river from Darnestown.*[75]

Right: Sergeant (later Captain) James May of the Fifteenth Massachusetts Infantry. *Collection of Ken Fleming.*

Below: Charge of the Fifteenth Massachusetts Infantry at Ball's Bluff. *Author's collection.*

Colonel Charles Devens of the Fifteenth Massachusetts Infantry. *Collection of Ken Fleming.*

Devens's men were still holding their line near the Jackson House when Lieutenant Howe arrived with the information that General Stone had issued new orders and that some cavalrymen were being sent to help Devens conduct further reconnaissance and maintain communication with Stone's headquarters. He also advised that Colonel Baker was now in overall command of the operation. While Colonel Devens's movements (forward and backward from his advanced line and then back again to the original position near the Jackson House) suggest that he was uncertain of what he was expected to do now that his force had been discovered, the absence of any orders from Baker to the contrary implied that Devens was expected to hold his position. It is likely, despite the shortage of boats, if Devens had broken off the engagement at this point, he could have retired to the safety of Harrison's Island with minimal loss. Colonel Devens was in a quandary, and no one seemed to know where Colonel Baker might be found to help clarify the situation.[76]

Colonel Devens sent Lieutenant Howe back down to the river with orders to locate Colonel Baker. On the shoreline, Howe found large numbers of men crossing over to the Virginia side but no sign of Baker. The cavalry that Devens was told to expect did arrive during this period but reported to Colonel Lee instead of to Devens. As Colonel Lee could not think of any orders for the mounted troopers, the officer in charge of the horsemen turned his men around and headed back over to Maryland. Confusion was rapidly taking hold of the operation on the bluff.

In his official report submitted after the battle, General Stone lamented:

> *For some reason never explained to me.... The cavalry were transferred to the Virginia shore, but were sent back without having left the shore to go inland, and thus Colonel Devens was deprived of the means of obtaining warning of any approach of the enemy. The battalion of Lieutenant-Colonel Ward was detained on the bluff in the rear of Colonel Devens, instead of being directed to the right.*[77]

Lieutenant Colonel Isaac Wistar. *Collection of Ken Fleming.*

Lieutenant Colonel Isaac J. Wistar was on the Maryland shore with nearly six hundred men of the California Regiment when the regimental chaplain rode up and told him that Colonel Baker desired the troops to cross over immediately. Wistar, who had been a law partner of Baker's before the war, needed little prodding. He ordered his men up and had six companies in the process of transport from Harrison's Island to the Virginia shoreline when he encountered Baker. When Baker (who was superbly mounted, having managed to get his horse over to the island on a flatboat) rode up, he shouted to Wistar, "Is that all the men you have got across?" Wistar responded that it was. Baker ordered the officer to "hurry all you can. Get everything that can float. Cross every man you can into Virginia." Baker's words suggested no equivocation. Although he had not yet set foot on Virginia soil, he was rapidly committing his entire force to the engagement.

While the Maryland and Virginia shorelines bustled with frantic activity, Lieutenant Colonel Ward's detachment of the Fifteenth Massachusetts reached Devens at his advanced position around 11:00 a.m. Although Devens had not ordered Ward up, he was glad to see him, as the regiment's strength was now filled out to about 650 men. Lieutenant Eager wrote that after the arrival of Ward's company, the next hour or so was marked by "occasional shots exchanged" between Union and Confederate pickets.[78] When the Confederate cavalryman Colonel Jenifer viewed the bolstered Union line, he determined that he would need reinforcements if he was to continue the fight. Jenifer sent back word to Colonel Evans. Concluding that the Union crossing at Edward's Ferry was merely a ruse, Evans shifted his full attention to the Union force on his left at Ball's Bluff. He called upon the capable Colonel Eppa Hunton and the Eighth Virginia Infantry (375 strong, but minus one company, left to guard the burned bridge) to move to Jenifer's support, telling them to drive the enemy to the river. The field of battle rapidly expanded as both sides brought men to the field.[79]

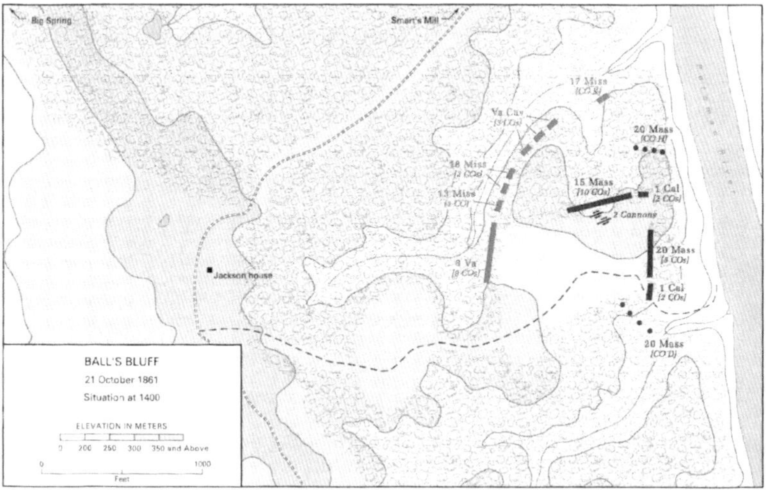

Positions of the opposing forces near Ball's Bluff (2:00 p.m.), October 21, 1861. *Center for Military History.*

The Eighth Virginia moved past Fort Evans then northward to join Jenifer's line near the Jackson House. Upon arriving, Colonel Hunton ordered his men into position in the fields south of the Jackson House, on the right of the Confederate line. The center of this line consisted of the four Mississippi companies, and on the left were the three companies of Virginia cavalry. Colonel Jenifer commanded the left and center elements of the force, while Hunton controlled the right. At about 12:30 p.m., the Confederates launched an attack on Devens's men. The Eighth Virginia, described by one Confederate officer as "375 people in bad temper" led the assault, with Colonel Hunton on horseback urging them on. A severe skirmish flared between the opposing lines, until Colonel Devens, fearing he was about to be flanked, broke off the engagement and withdrew. By 2:00 p.m., Devens had succeeded in bringing his bloodied command back to the cleared field at Ball's Bluff, where Colonel Lee and the Twentieth Massachusetts were waiting in support. The Twentieth Massachusetts was now at full strength, having been reinforced by Major Paul Revere (grandson of the Revolutionary War patriot) and the remaining companies of the regiment, which had been helping to bring artillery over from Harrison's Island. Colonel Lee had received no further orders from Colonel Baker, but he assumed that he was still to act in support of Devens. He placed his regiment in line along the top of the bluff facing west. Shortly after the men of the Twentieth fell into

Wounded in the fight. Private John Shafer Jr. of Company A, Eighth Virginia Infantry. *Collection of Ken Fleming.*

this line, they were joined by the artillery (two twelve-pound mountain howitzers of Battery B, First Rhode Island Light Artillery), which were carried up the slope with some difficulty and positioned in the cleared field in advance of Lee's men, on his right flank.

Quiet settled over the battlefield as the Fifteenth Massachusetts took position on the right flank of Colonel Lee's men facing south. Skirmishers from the Fifteenth and Twentieth Massachusetts were deployed in the woods to the north, in the rear of Devens's main line. The men of the Twentieth were eager to be tested, and in preparation, they took off their heavy, scarlet-lined wool overcoats and hung them in the branches of the trees behind them. Although the regimental historian later wrote that in the battle that followed the Confederates fired high volleys at these targets, ignoring the men drawn up in line of battle below, Lieutenant Abbott recalled the scene differently. He wrote to his parents on October 22, 1861, that the red lining of the coats was "so conspicuous as to draw the enemy's fire at a great rate. Though we were lying down, our men were shot on every side of us."[80]

Colonel Baker was still not on the field. Rather than investigate the ground upon which he was preparing to do battle, Baker remained on Harrison's Island, where he was engaged in trying to secure additional boats for troop transport. Baker had no shortage of troops, and they were now all jammed on Harrison's Island, trying to make their way across to the Virginia shoreline. Union officers reported that at no time were there more than seven boats (two flatboats, two small ferry boats, two skiffs and one metallic lifeboat) available to transport the troops across. Colonel Baker did little to bring order to the mayhem. Later it was revealed that he had spent more than four hours looking for boats and personally supervising the removal of a flatboat from the C&O Canal. This was an important duty to be sure but one that should have been more properly delegated to a staff officer. While Baker performed this task, Lieutenant Colonel Wistar and his First California Regiment, as well as the Tammany Regiment (Forty-Second New York) under Colonel Milton H. Cogswell arrived on Harrison's Island by about 1:00 p.m. Cogswell later reported great confusion on Harrison's Island and the Virginia shoreline, remembering: "No one seemed to be in charge, there was not anyone superintending the passage of the troops, and no order was maintained in their crossing."[81] Cogswell was an informed observer. A native of the Indiana frontier and born of rugged pioneer stock, he was also an experienced and professional soldier who had graduated from West Point in 1849 and served in the regular army.

A veteran of the Nineteenth Massachusetts Infantry who witnessed the Union crossing from Harrison's Island wrote of his baptism in war:

> *During the time occupied in ferrying the different commands to the island, the various regiments stood in line on the tow path, awaiting their turn. The Fifteenth Massachusetts, First California, Twentieth Massachusetts and some others had already crossed. The battle was in progress and wounded and dead men filled the places of the living as the scows returned for a new load. Standing thus, inactive, it was a sickening sight to see men with their heads, arms and legs tied up in bloody bandages and hear the groans of the poor fellows as they were helped out and slowly moved along the front of the regiments. The sight of a body of a soldier who had been killed, and the presence of so many wounded, had a disheartening effect upon many.*[82]

Back at Edward's Ferry, General Stone had little idea that such expanding resources were being directed toward the Virginia shore or that a battle line was being established in the cleared field atop the bluff. He had received no word from Colonel Baker but assumed that the operation was going well. At noon, Stone had sent Baker additional orders, passing along intelligence that had been received at headquarters. Baker encountered Colonel Cogswell and showed him Stone's message when he received it, about 1:30 p.m.:

> *I am informed that the force of the enemy is about 4,000, all told. If you push them, you may do so as far as to have a strong position near Leesburg, if you can keep them before you, avoiding their batteries. If they pass Leesburg and take the Gum Spring road you will not follow far, but seize the first good position to cover that road. Their design is to draw us on, if they are obliged to retreat, as far as Goose Creek, where they can be reinforced from Manassas and have a strong position. Report frequently, so that when they are pushed Gorman can come in on their flank.*[83]

Left: Colonel Milton Cogswell of the Tammany Regiment; *Right*: Union brigadier general Charles Stone. *Collection of Ken Fleming.*

Baker was still on Harrison's Island, and the purported size of the Confederate force did not seem to concern him. Baker reported back to Stone:

> *I acknowledge your order of 11:50, announcing their force at 4,000. I have lifted large boat out of the canal into the river. I shall, as soon as I feel strong enough, advance steadily, guarding my flanks carefully. I will communicate with you often.*[84]

It was the only message that Stone would ever receive from Colonel Baker.

Colonel Baker's communication is curious in a number of respects. Nowhere did Baker indicate that he had not yet personally crossed over to the Virginia shore or that he was not fully aware of the situation developing on the bluff. As Baker was only a short distance away, he must have heard the sounds of battle across the river, yet he did not acknowledge this fact or note any transportation problems. In sum, Baker expressed nothing but cautious optimism with regard to the operation. His communication suggested that there was little doubt regarding his ability to successfully press the Confederates. This feeling seemed to inspire Stone, who confidently telegraphed McClellan at 2:00 p.m.:

> *There has been sharp firing on the right of our line, and our troops appear to be advancing there under Baker. The left, under Gorman, has advanced its skirmishers nearly one mile, and if the movement continues successfully, will turn the enemy's right.*[85]

The Confederates were experiencing difficulties. Although Hunton's Virginians had caused Devens's men to fall back to the cleared field, the Virginians were running low on ammunition. Colonel Hunton dispatched a staff officer to Colonel Evans informing him of the situation. Evans told the officer to "tell Hunton to fight on" and dispatched Colonel Erasmus R. Burt with the remainder of the Eighteenth Mississippi Infantry to Ball's Bluff with orders to attack the Union left flank. Hunton continued to hold on, but at 3:30 p.m., he made a second appeal to Colonel Evans for more ammunition. Evans, who some fellow officers later accused of imbibing on this day, responded to this plea with words instead of bullets: "Tell Hunton to hold his ground till every damned man falls, I have sent him the Eighteenth [Mississippi Infantry] and will send him the Seventeenth."[86]

Private Benjamin Franklin Leith of Company E, Eighth Virginia Infantry. *Collection of Ken Fleming.*

Hunton's stunned staff officer was on his way back to the regiment, probably trying to think of a tactful way of relating this message to his colonel, when he observed a portion of the Eighth Virginia leaving the field. Riding forward, the officer asked if the regiment had been whipped. The officer commanding the detachment replied that he did not know, he had just been ordered to fall back. The staff officer found Colonel Hunton, relayed Evans's terse message and asked if the regiment had been ordered to retreat. Hunton was furious when he heard of the withdrawal and ordered his aide to bring the men back into line. This was accomplished with some difficulty over the next ninety minutes, as Hunton later noted that some of the men, being local boys and tired of the fight, simply left the battlefield and went home.[87]

Colonel Evans was acting decisively. Three months to the day that he had performed a similar bold maneuver at First Manassas, Evans divided his command once again. Retaining the Thirteenth Mississippi and one battery of the Richmond Howitzers at Fort Evans to hold Gorman's brigade in check, Evans shifted the bulk of his force to meet the Union threat on his left flank at Ball's Bluff. The Seventeenth and Eighteenth Mississippi (the former under Colonel W.S. Featherston) were ordered to march at double time toward Ball's Bluff. Evans was scrambling to bring as many men as possible into the battle, even going so far as to send a courier into Leesburg in an effort to mobilize the Loudoun militia. Although the militia could not be assembled, its commander, General R.L. Wright, and a few local men did report for action. Perhaps the most notable among these citizen-soldiers was Elijah Viers White, a swashbuckling twenty-nine-year-old who had ridden with Turner Ashby's Confederate partisans. He owned a large estate near Conrad's Ferry and knew the backroads of Loudoun County. A fierce fighter, White would prove invaluable to Colonel Evans as the colonel rushed his men into the fight at Ball's Bluff. In recognition of his distinguished service at Ball's Bluff, White was later commissioned a captain in the Confederate cavalry. By the end of the war, he had served as the lieutenant colonel of the Thirty-Fifth Virginia Cavalry ("The Comanches") and as the commander of the famed Laurel Brigade.

4

"One Blast Upon Your Bugle Horn"

Colonel Baker did not reach Ball's Bluff until about 2:15 p.m., and one of the first officers he saw upon arriving was Colonel Lee. Lee recalled that as he was directing his lines he heard his name called and looked over to see a striking silver-haired figure on horseback talking to Major Revere. The officer rode over to Lee, said, "I congratulate you on the prospect of a battle," and then bowed. It was Colonel Baker. Lee returned the bow and said, "I suppose you assume command."[88]

Colonel Baker may not have been a professional soldier, but in his splendidly tailored uniform and on his impressive mount, he knew how to make an entrance on the battlefield. Upon meeting Colonel Devens, Baker greeted him enthusiastically: "Colonel Devens, I congratulate you upon the splendid manner in which your regiment has behaved this morning. I think we better form the line here, and prepare to receive them here, and you shall have the right of the line."[89]

Although he had not yet personally surveyed the ground, Baker began to deploy the troops at hand. He had the troops from three regiments available to him: the Fifteenth and Twentieth Massachusetts and the First California Regiment. After the brief conversation with Devens, Baker ordered the Fifteenth Massachusetts to take position on the right flank of the new line he was forming. This line is historically remembered rather infamously as the L-shaped formation. It was, in retrospect, a tactically deficient arrangement that forced the regiments to face inward at right angles toward one another, with the two wings converging at the very edge of the bluff. The Fifteenth

Massachusetts and the California Regiment formed the shank of the L, and the Twentieth Massachusetts comprised the bar. Two companies of the Twentieth Massachusetts were deployed to cover the flanks, and two mountain howitzers were set on the right in front of the Fifteenth Massachusetts. It was a curious formation—the position assigned to the Fifteenth Massachusetts was on ground that gradually sloped away from the open field toward the river and the woods. The men posted here could barely see the position in front of them, and many of them simply sat down in the woods, feeling somewhat isolated from the main battle line. It was a position that offered no depth, with nothing but the cliffs of Ball's Bluff and the Potomac in its immediate rear.[90] The two California regiments on Devens's left also were in a bad spot and could not gain a clear view of their front since it was blocked by the converging right flank of the Twentieth Massachusetts.

Shortly after the battle, Lieutenant Henry Livermore Abbott of the Twentieth Massachusetts described the peculiar formation in a letter to his parents:

> *The uncovered space I have spoken of was the battleground. Part of Baker's brigade was drawn up on the right flank, on the edge of the wood, with the 15th. The rest was drawn across the opening, back towards the river, 30 feet from the top of the bank 15 feet behind them the 318 men of our regiment were drawn up in a second, parallel line, under command of Gen. Baker. The two howitzers* [were] *in front.*[91]

Baker was in trouble, but if he or any of the other high-ranking officers on the field recognized it, they gave little indication. Devens, who probably had the best understanding of the field, having traversed it during his various advances and withdrawals, was silent when Baker sought his counsel. Indeed, he was relieved that Baker was at least on the field and the responsibilities for the operation lifted from his shoulders. When he learned that Baker had arrived, Devens reportedly turned to his major and sighed, "Thank Heaven he has come. We have been waiting eight hours." He would later testify before a congressional committee to this effect, reflecting: "I had a very strong feeling of relief, of course, because I knew that from that moment I had nothing to do but fight my regiment; I had nothing to do with the tactics of the battle, or with anything except the minor tactics."[92]

Where hindsight would generate concern regarding Baker's decisions on the battlefield, as he considered his lines on the afternoon of October 21, 1861, Colonel Baker felt nothing but confidence in his tactical arrangements.

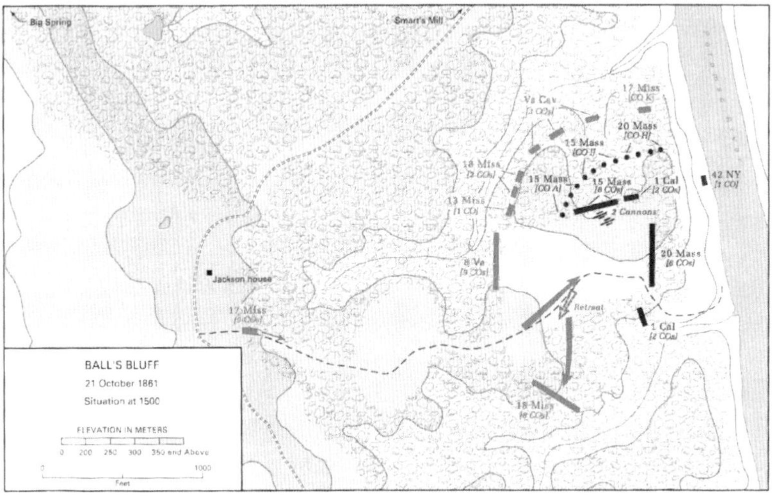

Action of Opposing Forces at Ball's Bluff (3:00 p.m.), October 21, 1861. *Center for Military History.*

His solicitation of the opinions of subordinate officers seems more indicative of Baker's intent to confirm the appropriateness of his command decisions than suggestive of any lack of self-confidence.

As the Union troops were establishing their new position on the bluff, elements of Jenifer's cavalry and the Eighth Virginia had trailed Devens when he fell back and taken position on the western side of the cleared field and in the woods to the north. Jenifer's dismounted cavalry moved cautiously through the woods and around the flank of the Fifteenth Massachusetts towards Devens's rear. Devens detected this movement and deployed skirmishers. His men were joined by some men from Company H of the Twentieth Massachusetts. Soon, a sharp fire erupted as the opposing forces met. Skirmishers of the Eighth Virginia began to rake the Union line with flanking fire. Back at Edward's Ferry, General Stone began to get word of heavy firing breaking out on the bluff. Assuming that Baker had started his advance, Stone telegraphed McClellan to advise: "There has been sharp fighting on the right of our line, and our troops appear to be advancing there under Baker. The left, under Gorman, has advanced its skirmishers nearly 1 mile, and, if the movement continues successful, will turn the enemy's right." If ever in the history of warfare situational understanding was clouded by the fog of battle, this message from Stone to McClellan could serve as a striking

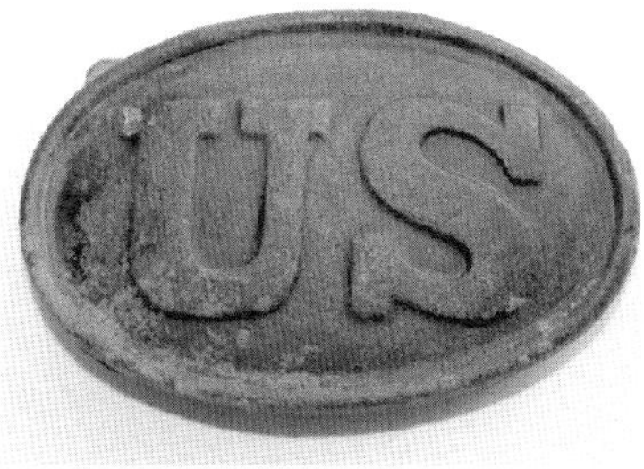

U.S. belt plate Recovered from Lines of the Twentieth Massachusetts Infantry at Ball's Bluff. *Author's collection.*

example. Upon receipt, McClellan enthusiastically responded with a coded message: "Take Leesburg." When the message arrived at Stone's headquarters, it was discovered that Stone did not have the key to decipher the communication. He sent an urgent, but cryptic, message back to McClellan: "I have the key, but don't have the box."[93]

While the situation atop Ball's Bluff was developing, Stone had sent three infantry regiments from Gorman's brigade across the Potomac at Edward's Ferry. These troops were expected to come in on the right flank of the Confederates, but only a few of Gorman's troops advanced and remained about a mile from the ferry. The Confederates felt no threat on their right flank.

At about 2:30 p.m., Colonel Milton Cogswell and one company of the Tammany Regiment crossed over from Harrison's Island to the Virginia shore. Cogswell was accompanied by one of the rifled James guns of the Rhode Island battery; his men were able to get it to the top of the bluff but with great difficulty. When Cogswell reached the crest, he encountered Colonel Baker. Once again, as soon as Baker saw him, he recited poetry, this time paraphrasing Sir Walter Scott's poem *The Lady of the Lake* and exhorting: "One blast upon your bugle horn/Is worth a thousand men."[94] The moment for poetry past, the officers got down to the business of war and walked over to Lieutenant Colonel Wistar's position on the southeast corner of the field. Sporadic small arms fire could be heard, and Baker suggested that the officers stay low to the ground to avoid getting hit. Cogswell expressed concerns about some high ground near a wooded ravine on the Union flank that was currently unoccupied but would compromise the Union position if the Confederates were able to secure it. The three officers also discussed Stone's estimates of 4,000 Confederates opposing them, and Wistar opined that because of the long delay in the transmittal of Stone's message, the Confederates had likely reached full strength on his front. Wistar believed that the Confederate force might actually number as many as 5,000 to 7,000 men. Baker understood Wistar's concerns but said that the only way to determine for sure what was on their front was to deploy skirmishers. He ordered Cogswell to take command of the artillery and directed Wistar to send out two companies from his regiment. Wistar thought the order misguided and believed his men would get slaughtered if they ran into a large force of the enemy, but he complied. At about 3:00 p.m., he sent out two companies (about 150 men) under the command of Captain John Markoe. Just as these men entered the woods, the waiting Eighth Virginia Infantry rose up and unleashed a devastating volley into Markoe's right flank. Short on ammunition, they followed the volley with a bayonet charge. Wistar's men returned fire and fell back to the wood line on the south side of the field.[95]

Captain Francis G. Young, an officer serving as quartermaster on Baker's staff, described the fight:

> *When our skirmishing companies had reached the edge of the woods, suddenly the enemy hitherto concealed began fighting in their usual manner, first giving a yell and volley, then loading and firing at will for a few minutes, then ceasing an equal time; then giving another yell and volley, and so on, pouring a murderous fire into our little band for the space of half an hour. The whole woods swarmed with them.... We kept up both a musketry and cannon fire as well as we could, but half the time we could not see the enemy, and his cowardly discharges were thinning our ranks, still most of the men stood firm and acted bravely. The enemy's volleys and yells increased in loudness, and it was evident that reinforcements were pouring in to his aid.*[96]

Lieutenant James Jackson Lowell, Company E, Twentieth Massachusetts Infantry. *Collection of Ken Fleming.*

Because his two companies were shorthanded, Lieutenant Colonel Wistar had accompanied Markoe's scouting party into the woods. When the Virginians engaged his force and then began expanding their fire toward the main body of Union troops on the bluff, Wistar gave over immediate command to Captain Markoe and "ran back as hard as [he] could to take command of [the] regiment."[97] Markoe's small force fought valiantly but was outnumbered. Markoe went down with a serious shoulder wound and was captured. All of the other officers were killed, and the force pulled back to the main line, firing as they retreated. By the time what was left of Markoe's bloodied force staggered back into to Wistar's main line of defense, it was about 3:30 p.m.

Colonel Evans had determined to fight this battle on the bluff and directed his forces to concentrate there. The firing on the bluff continued, as the Eighth Virginia pulled back in confusion and was replaced in line by eight companies of Colonel Erasmus Burt's Eighteenth Mississippi and nine companies of Colonel Featherston's Seventeenth Mississippi. Featherston's men slipped in on the right flank of the Eighth Virginia, which continued to try and pick off the gunners manning the two Howitzers posted out in the open field near the Twentieth Massachusetts. Burt's Eighteenth Mississippi joined in this fire on the guns and then charged them, forcing the Union artillerymen to pull their guns back into the cover of the woods. Captain Lorenzo D. Fletcher of the Thirteenth Mississippi Infantry described the action in his report of the battle:

> *Upon my arrival my company was thrown forward into the field side by side with the Eighth Virginia Regiment and a part of the Eighteenth Mississippi Regiment, who had come up also, under the command of Major E.G. Henry. Then it was that quite a spirited and hot contest ensued, in which my company acted a conspicuous part. The enemy having a position near a battery of howitzers, an order was given to charge the battery, which was responded to instantly by my company and the Virginians, and I think a portion of the Eighteenth Mississippi. The charge was successful, the guns were taken, several of my men among the first to reach the guns and take part in their removal. In the charge I suffered no loss except one man fell mortally wounded, having been shot through the breast while making his way to the guns. At the time he fell he was among the farthest in advance.*[98]

Unfortunately, Colonel Burt, riding on horseback, had made a grave tactical error and led his men directly between the two wings of the Union position. He was mortally wounded in the charge, suffering a severe wound to his hip. Lieutenant Colonel Thomas Griffin assumed command of the regiment as it fell back to the original wood line from where it had initiated the attack. Lieutenant Colonel Griffin adjusted his line, detaching two companies to extend his left flank to fill a gap between his regiment and the Eighth Virginia and directed another two companies to the right to deal with the two companies of the California Regiment that still remained on the south side of the field. Despite the huge gap that this move created in the Confederate line, Baker and the other Union officers on the bluff were so focused on the defensive they failed to exploit the tactical opportunity.

Captain (later Major) George Macy, Twentieth Massachusetts. *Henry Deeks Collection.*

Eventually, the Confederates realized the weakness of their deployment and filled the gap with Colonel Featherston's Seventeenth Mississippi.

As the Eighth Virginia and the Mississippi troops were making their attacks, Colonel Cogswell had ordered the rifled six-pounder James gun into action and positioned it near the Twentieth Massachusetts. He personally directed its fire, but the Confederates were well protected in the woods and endured the artillery fire without loss. In response, Confederate skirmishers moved forward and methodically picked off the Union gunners and killed or wounded most of the battery horses. At one point in the fight, Cogswell, Wistar and Baker personally manned the gun, but the heavy Confederate fire rendered their efforts useless. After only a short time, the gun was abandoned. In the haste of battle, however, the green artillerists had neglected to unlimber the gun—that is, detach it from the horses and its train—and the wounded and spooked horses careened through the ranks of the Twentieth Massachusetts. This created great disorder in the regiment's line of battle. A few brave men endured the enemy fire and were able to separate the horses from the gun, but the limber eventually ended up tumbling down the bluff toward the river. The striking image of the cannon coming down the side of the bluff made a deep impression on a member of the Nineteenth Massachusetts, who remembered the scene fifty-five years later. His regiment had assembled on the shore of Harrison's Island "just in time to see a little 12-pounder, which had been carried up to the bluff, spiked and tumbled over the cliff into the river. It had done valiant work but all except two of its crew had been killed or disabled and in no other way than by destroying it could the fleeing men save it from falling into the hands of the confederates."[99] In truth, during the fight, the gun had fired only ten rounds, and now all of the Union artillery on the Bluff had been silenced, with hardly any men available to service the guns.

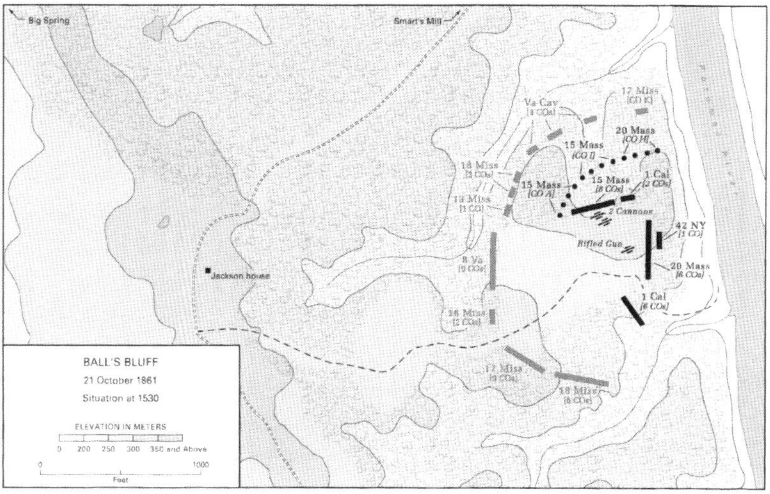

Action of opposing forces at Ball's Bluff (3:30 p.m.), October 21, 1861. *Center for Military History.*

The battle on the bluff was intensifying, and the late afternoon was taken by a series of small, but significant, actions all along the line. The California Regiment was running short on ammunition. Armed with old .69-caliber smoothbore flintlock muskets that had been converted to percussion, the soldiers scavenged the Confederate dead and were able to secure additional rounds from discarded cartridge boxes. Hunton's Virginians and Jenifer's cavalry also were running low and sent back word to Colonel Evans for both ammunition and provisions.

Baker's force was in a precarious spot. Between 4:30 and 5:00 p.m., under heavy pressure from the Confederates, he was barely holding on to his position. There was heavy firing all across the line, but it was particularly fierce on Baker's left. On the western edge of the cleared field, the Confederates laid down a steady fire that forced the Twentieth Massachusetts to fall back into the woods. In the confused fight that raged here, Lieutenant Colonel Wistar went down with his third and most serious wound of the day. The impact of the bullet knocked him from his feet and left him crumpled on the ground. The bullet had struck him in the right elbow, shattering "all three of the bones meeting at that point, causing a momentary mental confusion and even suspension of sight."[100] It was a wound that would take him out of the fight. Colonel Baker rushed to his friend and helped him to his feet. He picked up Wistar's sword and sheathed it before calling to a soldier in

Unidentified soldier of the California Regiment. *Author's collection.*

the California Regiment and directing him to assist Lieutenant Colonel Wistar in getting down to the river. After saying his farewell to Wistar, Baker proceeded to walk up and down the left end of the Union line, making a heroic show for his men—his ornate presentation sword in one hand, the other thrust into the breast of his frock coat. At one point, he remarked to an officer standing nearby, "The officer who dies with his men will never be harshly judged." Although the men were calling for Baker to take cover, Baker ignored their pleas, sharply responding to one officer who expressed concern: "You attend to Company G. I will look after myself."[101]

During this same action, Lieutenant Colonel Ward of the Fifteenth Massachusetts went down with a bullet in his left leg. A surgeon recalled that Ward's leg had been "shattered by a huge musket ball which passed through sideways."[102] Ward was removed to a hospital set up in a house on Harrison's Island, where he endured painful amputation. The loss of his leg would not dampen Ward's dedication to duty. He would get fitted for a prosthetic limb, be promoted to the rank of colonel and return to his regiment to lead it at Gettysburg just eight months later. At Gettysburg, on the afternoon of July 2, 1863, while trying to rally his men, Ward was mortally wounded by a shell fragment that tore into his right leg and severed an artery. After remaining out on the battlefield for the better part of a day and suffering extensive blood loss, Ward was found by his brother, who also served in the regiment, and carried to a field hospital. Lieutenant Colonel Ward died the next day. In the months before Ball's Bluff, Ward had written in a letter to his wife back home in Worcester: "I would like very much to see you, but probably shall not very soon. I am bound for the fight, when it comes, and I trust I shall never disgrace myself or my friends, by any cowardly, or unmanly act."[103]

Lieutenant Oliver Wendell Holmes Jr. of the Twentieth Massachusetts suffered multiple wounds during this part of the fight. The first bullet hit him in the stomach without breaking the skin, and Holmes later described

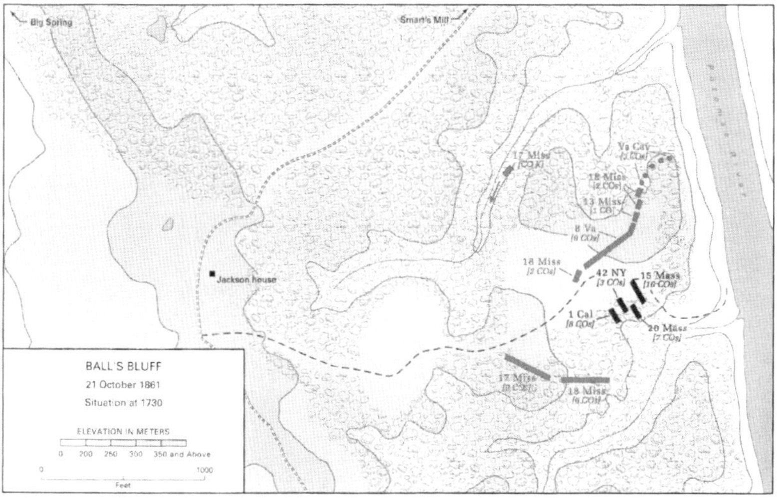

Above: Action of opposing forces at Ball's Bluff (5:30 p.m.), October 21, 1861. *Center for Military History.*

Right: Lieutenant Oliver Wendell Holmes, Twentieth Massachusetts. *Steve Meadow Collection.*

the wound: "I felt as if a horse had kicked me." In a remarkable letter to his mother dated October 23, 1861, sent from a regimental field hospital, Holmes wrote that he was "out in front of our men encouraging 'em when a spent shell knocked the wind out of me and I fell." Holmes then began crawling toward to rear with the help of a comrade. Colonel Devens saw him and commented, "That's right Mr. Holmes—Go to the Rear." In his letter, Holmes confessed that after realizing his wound was not so serious, he believed his most appropriate place was with his men. He rose to his feet and then raised his sword over his head and asked his men if they were willing to follow him forward into the fight. He was standing next to Devens in this attempt to rally his men when he was struck by another bullet—this time more seriously. Holmes was carried down to the base of the bluff by Sergeant Henry Smith.[104] The bullet had struck Holmes in the breast, and he later admitted to a friend, "I thought I was a gone coon." Sergeant Smith opened Holmes's shirt to reveal the wound and used his fingers to squeeze the bullet free. As he awaited transport to Harrison's Island, the literary-minded Holmes pondered his condition, remembering a character in one of his favorite childhood books who, having been shot in the lungs, died in terrible agony. It was not a pleasant thought, and Holmes was thankful for the small bottle of laudanum he had brought with him from home to deal with just this sort of circumstance. Holmes was ferried across the Potomac and carried to a small log house on Harrison's Island that was piled with moaning wounded. Although he frequently fingered the bottle of laudanum, he was reluctant to use it and decided to await the surgeon's decision on the seriousness of his wound and save the drug in case the pain later became unbearable. Holmes wrote: "I didn't feel sure there was no chance—and watching myself did not feel the hand of death upon me beyond a hope—my strength seemed to hold out too well." Holmes survived his wound (and another suffered later at Antietam) and lived on to become one of the most distinguished jurists to ever serve on the United States Supreme Court.[105]

Lieutenant Willie Putnam, Twentieth Massachusetts Infantry, killed at Ball's Bluff. *Author's collection.*

Holmes's cousin Lieutenant Willie Putnam was not as lucky. During the fight, Putnam had rushed forward to help one of his men and received a grave wound to his abdomen. He lingered in excruciating pain for a day—treating his own wounds due the shortage of doctors—as his intestines were protruding from his gut. When medical attention did arrive, he refused it, encouraging them instead to treat those with fairer prospects of survival. Sadly, the tragedy would claim more than the young officer. Back in Boston, less than two months after receiving word of his son's passing, Putnam's father, Samuel R. Putnam, a retired merchant, died at his residence.[106]

Casualties continued to mount in the ranks of the two Massachusetts regiments. The surnames of the dead and wounded were those of the nation's most noteworthy founding families. Young men whose forefathers had settled New England as Pilgrims, signed the Declaration of Independence under the threat of treason or helped forge the new nation in the fires of the revolution, now lay bleeding and dying on a Virginia battlefield of a nation rent by civil war.

Remembering the battle, Lieutenant Abbott wrote that "the fight was made up of charges. You would see capt[ain]s rush out in front & cry forward & their companies would follow them at full speed under a tremendous fire till they were obliged to fall back….[T]his was repeated over and over during the 4 hours fight."[107] Captain Bartlett of the Twentieth Massachusetts wrote with mixed emotions about ferocity of the fight:

> [T]*he first volley came and the bullets flew like hail….The men now began to drop around me; most of them were lying down in the first of it, being ordered to keep in reserve. Those that were lying down, if they lifted their foot or head it was struck. One poor fellow near me was struck in the hip while lying flat, and rose to go to the rear, when another struck him on the head and knocked him over. I felt that I was going to be hit, I should be, whether I stood up or lay down, so I stood up and walked around, stepping over them and talking to them in a joking way, to take their thoughts away from the bullets, and keep them more self-possessed. I was surprised at first at my own coolness. I never felt better, although I expected of course that I should feel the lead every second, and I was wondering where it would take me. I kept speaking to Lit* [Henry L. Abbott], *surprised that he was not hit amongst the rain of bullets. I said two or three times "Why Lit, aren't you hit yet?"…Lit was as cool and brave as I knew he would be. The different companies began to wilt away under this terrible fire.*[108]

Captain Caspar Crowinshield, a twenty-three-year-old officer serving with the Twentieth Massachusetts also described the hectic scene, writing in a letter to his mother one day after the battle:

> *At 1 o'clk the fight Commenced on our right flank and in a short time the rebels were driven back. Then Came a breathing space of 10 minutes. Then they attacked our left flank. Where I was they made a dreadful noise and fired heavily and rapidly. They drove my pickets in and killed at the 1st fire 2 or 3 men. My men stood firm and fought bravely. I was obliged to bring up a reserve, and we drove the rebels back. An interval of quiet, and they advanced cheering & attacking our whole line. We met them with a severe fire and they fell back, but they Continued to fire very rapidly, and killed many of our mem. They cheered furiously, as their reinforcements came up, and their fire became fiercer & fiercer.*[109]

The fighting raged so furiously that a private in the Twentieth Massachusetts took aim at a Confederate officer and was surprised to find that he could not pull the trigger of his rifle because his finger had been clipped off cleanly at the joint.[110]

Following the swirl of actions in the cleared field, the men of the Eighteenth Mississippi fell back to the woods and took position on the high wooded ridge that bordered the south side of the field. It was the same position that had been identified by Lieutenant Colonel Wistar earlier in the fight but had remained unsecured. The Confederates continued moving east along this ridgeline until they reached a point overlooking the river. It was at this point that they were discovered and were engaged by mixed companies of the Tammany and California Regiments. The Mississippians advanced at least five times but were repulsed in desperate fighting that stopped them in their tracks.

The Union line was being severely pressed, and many of the officers began to fear that the position could not be held. The men were hungry and exhausted; many had been on the field since dawn. In addition, the fighting was taking its toll on the command structure, as a great number of officers were down and out of the fight. While the Union officers considered the current state of affairs (and were no doubt thinking about the lack of sufficient boats to make a safe retreat), the Confederates were aggressively advancing the offensive. The cavalrymen under Colonel Jenifer were slowly working their way east on the Union right flank, toward the base of Ball's Bluff. If possible, Jenifer hoped to block any escape route to the north along

Lithographic depiction of Colonel Baker's death. *Author's collection.*

the river to Smart's Mill Ford should the Union force be pushed down to the Potomac shoreline. In effect, the Union position was slowly becoming encircled by the Confederates, who were forcing the Union line contract with every step of their advance. A Massachusetts soldier wrote: "We were driven back inch by inch towards the top of the bank."[111]

It was at this point that the course of battle took a critical turn: as Colonel Baker was walking the line, he was wounded. There are many conflicting and varying accounts of how many times Baker was hit.[112] Captain Francis G. Young of Baker's staff claimed, "One man rode forward, presented a revolver at Baker, and fired all its charges at him. Our gallant leader fell, and at the same moment all our lines were driven back by the overwhelming force opposed to them."[113] Another Union officer said that it was the Confederate colonel E.R. Burt himself who fired the fatal shots.[114] Captain Crowinshield of the Twentieth Massachusetts, perhaps the most reliable of the witnesses on the field who left a contemporary account, wrote that he was standing

Captain Louis Bieral of the First California Regiment. *Author's collection.*

next to Baker when he was hit by "3 or 4 bullets." To the captain's horror Baker fell, struggled to regain his footing and then fell again.[115] Crowinshield was splattered with Baker's blood and brains. Baker was struck by anywhere from three to nine bullets depending on various accounts. A newspaper correspondent who later viewed Baker's body in Poolesville reported that "one of the bullets penetrated the head just below the left ear, another entered the right side of the throat, a third had apparently passed his left arm and penetrated his heart, a fourth penetrated his abdomen, and the lower extremities were ball-riven all over."[116]

A swarm of Confederates surged forward to capture Baker's sword, but Captain Young called upon the men to go to their fallen colonel's defense. Captain Winthrop of the Nineteenth Massachusetts wrote that "there was a hand to hand struggle over [Baker's] dead body, but that it was rescued by his men and tenderly borne to the rear."[117] This party of Union soldiers was led by Captain Louis Bieral of the California Regiment, who charged forward and shot a Confederate who was bending over Baker's body. Bieral was wounded several times during the fight, including one injury sustained as a result of being struck by the butt of a Confederate musket in the testicles—evidence of the ferocity and desperate close quarters of the fight.[118] Captain Young and Baker's nephew Lieutenant Edward Jerome carried Baker's body down the bluff and placed it in a flatboat bound for Harrison's Island with the dead and wounded.[119]

Baker's death marked a turning point in the battle. Captain Young told a *New York Tribune* reporter that when he reached Harrison's Island, he looked over toward the Virginia shore and "saw such a spectacle as no tongue can describe. Our entire forces were retreating, tumbling, rolling, leaping down the steep heights, the enemy following, murdering, and taking prisoners."[120] Baker's death also affected the morale of the Union reserve troops on Harrison's Island who were in the process of crossing over to the Virginia side to reinforce the Union position. As the boat carrying Baker's body reached Harrison's Island, the untested infantrymen of the

Steel engraving depicting the death of Colonel Baker. *Author's collection.*

Nineteenth Massachusetts stood stunned. In describing the moment, the regimental historian dryly noted: "This incident had a demoralizing effect on the men."[121]

Captain Winthrop of the 19th Massachusetts was one of those men. In 1889, he wrote of Baker: "His was the first face of a dead soldier killed in action that I had ever looked upon. His body was carried past the flank of my company as we were forming in line of battle on Harrison's Island, and I stepped from the ranks and turned back the military cloak that covered it. That face has a place in my memory yet—calm, noble, majestic, his gray hair stained with blood. He had displayed the grandest courage of all through the fight."[122]

Another veteran of the Nineteenth Massachusetts Infantry recalled watching as Baker's body was brought over to Harrison's Island:

> *Instinctively there was a hush along the entire line, and hats were raised as the body of* [Colonel] *Baker, covered with an American flag, was tenderly lifted out of the scow and slowly borne along the front. This incident had almost a demoralizing effect, but the command to "Pile in lively, boys" occupied the attention at once and the men of the Nineteenth jumped into the*

Left: Illustrated song sheet dedicated to Colonel Baker. *Author's collection.*

Below: Memorial envelope published after Colonel Baker's Death. *Author's collection.*

Opposite: Tattered battle flags of the Nineteenth Massachusetts Infantry. *Library of Congress.*

> *scow and hauled it over to the island just as dusk* [descended]. *Company F, being the left flank company, was the last to cross, and the sight of Baker's body had angered the men that as they poled their boat over, they sang with vigor, "We'll hang Jeff Davis to a Sour Apple Tree."*[123]

Ironically, while the Union force at Ball's Bluff was poised on the brink of disaster, General Stone, who remained at Edward's Ferry, had every reason to believe that things were going smoothly. He had received no communication from Colonel Baker since 1:30 p.m. and assumed that all was going well. In fact, while the Union troops were struggling to maintain their position at Ball's Bluff and were on the verge of being pushed into the Potomac, McClellan, who had even less knowledge of the operation than Stone, was thinking that the operation should be expanded to include a move to take Leesburg. McClellan telegraphed these intentions to Stone, who, still believing that McCall was moving toward the town from Dranesville (McClellan had neglected to inform Stone to the contrary), replied: "I believe this command can occupy Leesburg to-day." Stone ended his communication on a cautionary note, stating that "we are a little short of boats."[124] Tragically, his words would prove to be one of the great understatements of the war.

5

Panic on the Bluff

The death of Colonel Baker created a crisis in the Union command at Ball's Bluff. Given the confusion of battle, however, only those soldiers in proximity to Baker when he was struck or who saw his body carried from the field realized that he had been killed. The most immediate question raised by his death was the issue of who was now in command. Colonel Lee believed he was the most senior officer on the field and began to confer with Colonel Devens about tactical options. The two officers agreed that the battle was lost and were in the process of preparing orders for a general withdrawal across the Potomac when Colonel Cogswell came up. Cogswell was a man on a mission, having been informed by Captain Frederick Harvey, who was one of Baker's staff officers, that Colonels Lee and Devens were in a council of war preparing for a retreat. Devens later recalled that he reported to Colonel Lee to receive orders, and that, upon meeting with Lee, the colonel expressed "his opinion that the only thing to be done was to retreat to the river, and that the battle was utterly lost."[125] Cogswell insisted to both officers that he was in command of the field and did not support a general retreat. Cogswell reasoned that an orderly withdrawal across the Potomac was not possible given the shortage of boats and the pressure being exerted by the Confederates. Colonel Lee agreed to abide by Cogswell's assertion of command and listened as Cogswell argued that the only recourse available to the Union troops was to attempt to cut their way through the Confederates to Edward's Ferry, where Gorman's Brigade was waiting.[126]

Woodcut of retreat from Ball's Bluff. *Author's collection.*

Controversy raged for many years after the battle as to who was responsible for the order to retreat. Writing for the *National Tribune* newspaper in 1893, Eugene Sullivan, who served as a private in the Tammany Regiment, criticized the tenuous position in which Colonel Devens had put the Union forces at Ball's Bluff and defended his own colonel's (Cogswell) decision to withdraw from the fight. He noted that upon

> *taking command, Col. Cogswell, instead of ordering a retreat, endeavored to rally around him the now panic-stricken troops, which were going in all directions but that of the enemy, and seeing that all was lost, and capture by the enemy unavoidable, unless some desperate effort was made to keep back the enemy. Col. Cogswell resolved to try the only honorable and soldierly course left open to him, which was that of endeavoring to cut his way through what he considered the weakest point of the line on our left flank, and if possible get to Edward's Ferry, which was about three miles lower down the river, with what men he could take with him.*[127]

At this point in the battle, there were few choices available to the beleaguered Union force, but Cogswell was asking much of soldiers who had

Left: Colonel Milton Cogswell of the Tammany Regiment. *Library of Congress*.

Right: Drowned in the Potomac. Corporal William Tanner of the First Rhode Island Light Artillery. *Collection of Ken Fleming*.

been fighting all day and were short on both ammunition and provisions. Cogswell's breakout plan was bold and desperate but likely the only option save mass surrender or a pell-mell, "every man for himself" retreat across the Potomac back to Harrison's Island.

In order to accomplish his breakout plan, Cogswell ordered Colonel Devens to shift the Fifteenth Massachusetts from the Union right to a position in the rear of the Twentieth Massachusetts. After this move was completed, the Fifteenth would then advance in a column of assault against the Mississippians gathered on the Union left. This realignment of the Union position, however, was observed by the men of the Eighth Virginia. They were running desperately low on ammunition but saw an opportunity to take advantage. Colonel Hunton ordered a distribution of the available ammunition to ensure that each soldier had at least one round in his musket. After ordering his men to fix bayonets, Hunton led them forward. The Virginians charged across the open field and were met by two companies of the Twentieth Massachusetts. The Union companies were compelled to retire and give up the two silenced howitzer cannon that sat exposed near their lines.

The loss of these two guns offers another interesting footnote to the story of Ball's Bluff. Several accounts of the battle describe the service of an African American soldier who fought with the Massachusetts troops. This individual was almost certainly Louis A. Bell, a freed slave from Ohio, who worked as a paid servant to Colonel Cogswell. One account indicates that the Confederates were so furious at Bell's presence on the battlefield in a "semi-military" uniform that they fired on Union soldiers near the howitzers who had signaled their intent to surrender. The account recalled that "a lusty negro, with brazen front, stood armed in the ranks" and was more "than our men could bear." Louis Bell was taken prisoner at Ball's Bluff and sent to Richmond with the other men captured in the battle. Newspaper accounts indicate that Bell was released from prison in February 1862, but no further information about his fate appears in the historical record.[128]

In the Union breakout maneuver, Devens's men were to be supported by several companies detached from the Tammany and California Regiments, which were already on the Union left flank. In practice, however, these movements did not work out as smoothly as anticipated by Cogswell. The Massachusetts men did not fully advance on Cogwell's order. Colonel Devens described the movement in his report of the battle:

> *Confusion was created by the appearance of an officer of the enemy's in front of the companies of the Tammany Regiment who called on them to charge on the enemy. The detachment of the Tammany Regiment, probably mistaking this for an order from their own officers, rushed forward to the charge and a part of the 15th Massachusetts supposing that an order had been given for the advance of the whole line, rushed forward with eagerness, but was promptly recalled by their officers who had received no such order. The Rebels drove back the Tammany companies which retreated in such a way as to produce considerate confusion.*[129]

The identity of this mysterious "Confederate" officer has long perplexed historians of the Ball's Bluff fight. Long after the war, while giving a speech in dedication of a monument to the Confederate soldiers of Loudoun County, Elijah White asserted that this officer was Lieutenant Charles Wildman, who was serving as a staff officer to Colonel Evans at Ball's Bluff. Wildman's purported role also found its way into Colonel Hunton's memoirs as well as several recent histories of the battle. Closer inspection of the historical record, however, would suggest that Wildman was not the officer referred to in Colonel Devens's report and that the officer in question was actually Colonel Cogswell of the Tammany Regiment.[130]

Cogswell was captured toward the close of the battle and did not file his battle report until nearly a year later. During the intervening period, the issue of the Confederate officer who tried to "deceive" the Union troops at Ball's Bluff was all but forgotten, overshadowed by other controversies at later fights such as Shiloh and the Seven Days' battles. Cogswell's report is worth noting, however, for its clarification of one aspect of the history of Ball's Bluff that has long proved puzzling. Cogswell wrote that, having given orders for the movement toward Edward's Ferry, he "proceeded to the front, and finding our lines pressed severely…ordered an advance of the whole force on the right of the enemy line." He continued, "I was followed by the remnants of my two companies and a portion of the California Regiment, but, for some reason unknown to me, was not joined by either the Fifteenth or the Twentieth Massachusetts Regiments."[131]

Colonel Cogswell's exhortations to the Massachusetts men were observed by many officers on the field who, in the confusion of battle, likely believed that he was a Confederate officer attempting to lead the Union soldiers into an ambush. Cogswell makes no mention of any mounted Confederate officer in his report or any attempted ruse by the enemy while accepting full responsibility for ordering the attack in which he reported the Fifteenth and Twentieth Massachusetts did not participate. The conclusion that Cogswell was the officer so many mistook for a Confederate gains further credence when one considers an account from one of the Tammany soldiers. In this published account, Private Eugene Sullivan of Company K of the Forty-Second New York wrote that the Tammany men were wearing the "regimental uniform gray, with black facings."[132] While Colonel Cogswell was likely wearing a standard officer's double-breasted uniform of dark blue/black coloration, he was standing before troops clad in gray uniforms. An account of the Ball's Bluff fight published in a New York newspaper shortly after the battle reported that Captain O'Meara of the Tammany Regiment was wearing "the old gray uniform furnished [to the regiment] at Great Neck [New York], which bears a strong resemblance to the uniforms usually worn in Secessia. So complete was the similarity that a Confederate officer mistook him for one of their number."[133] The idea that a Confederate officer might appear on the battlefield and try to lead Union troops into ambush certainly stirred the fertile imaginations of rank-and-file soldiers. The imagery was promoted by purveyors of popular opinion as evidence of the Confederacy's failure to adhere to the established rules of warfare. The

Civil War has long been referred to as the war of the Blue and the Gray, but in the early months of the conflict, there was an interchangeable variety to the color of the uniforms worn by each side. In fact, at Ball's Bluff, the men of Company B, Seventeenth Mississippi, wore blue shirts to distinguish them from the other companies in their regiment.[134]

When Cogswell's men charged forward at about 6:00 p.m., the Seventeenth and Eighteenth Mississippi, along with some men from the Eighth Virginia, met the challenge. The Seventeenth Mississippi launched a counterattack that sent the disjointed Union advance reeling. Lieutenant Colonel John McGuirk of the Seventeenth Mississippi described the scene:

> *The men manifested confidence under the coolness of their officers. They seemed fighting a sham battle, when above the roar of musketry was heard the command of Colonel Featherston, "Charge, Mississippians, charge! Drive them into the Potomac or into eternity!" The sound of his voice seemed to echo from the vales of Maryland. The line arose as one man from a kneeling posture, discharged a deadly volley advanced the crescent line, and thus encircled the invaders, who in terror called for quarter and surrendered.*

Another officer of the Seventeenth Mississippi, admiring the tenacity of the Union soldiers, observed: "The Federal force fought well. A number were killed with the bayonet by my men."[135]

Panic spread through the disjointed Union ranks as the line faltered and then fell backward. Colonel Cogswell tried to organize a defensive line, but the Confederates proved too much for his men. The Tammany soldiers were pushed back in confusion and disorder and tumbled into and through the lines of Fifteenth Massachusetts. Lieutenant Abbott of the Twentieth Massachusetts wrote, "[W]e found the whole regiment cut to pieces & broken up…& Col. Lee sitting under a tree, swearing he wouldn't go another step, but had rather be taken prisoner."[136] Private Randolph Shotwell, a seventeen-year-old private in the Eighth Virginia, did not personally take part in his regiment's pursuit of the Union soldiers to the bluff but left a stirring account of the action that conforms to other eyewitness accounts. Long after the war, the literary-minded Shotwell published a memoir of his service:

> *Then ensued an awful spectacle! A kind of shiver ran through the huddled mass upon the brow of the cliff; it gave way, rushed a few steps; then in*

one wild panic stricken herd, rolled, leaped, tumbled over the precipice. The descent is nearly perpendicular, with ragged, jutting crags, and a water laved base. Screams of pain and terror filled the air. Men seemed suddenly bereft of reason, they leaped over the bluff with muskets still in their clutch, threw themselves into the river without divesting themselves of their heavy accoutrements, hence went to the bottom like lead. Others sprang down upon the heads and bayonets of those below. A gray-haired private of the 1st California was found with his head mashed between two rocks by the heavy boots of a ponderous "Tammany" man, who had broken his own neck by the fall! The side of the bluff was worn smooth by the number sliding down.

From the beginning of the battle a steady stream of wounded men had been trickling down the zig-zag path heading to the narrow beach, whence the boats were to convey them to the Island. As it happened the two larger bateaux were just starting with an overload when the torrent of terror-stricken fugitives rolled down the bluffs upon them. Both boats were instantly submerged, and their cargoes of helpless human beings (crippled by wounds) were swept away to unknown graves. The whole surface of the river seemed filled with heads, struggling, screaming, fighting, dying: Man clutched at man, and the strong who might have escaped were dragged down by the weaker. Voices that strove to shout for help were stifled by the turbid waters of the swollen river and died away in gurgles. It is strange how persons about to drown turn to their fellows for strength; they may be in mid-ocean, with no hope for any, yet they grasp one another and sink in pairs. Captain Otter of the 1st California (an opposite [sic] *name for a swimmer) was found a few days later with two men of his company clutching his neckband. Had he attempted to save them, or had they seized him and dragged him down? One officer was found with $126 in gold in his pocket: it had cost his life.*[137]

Lieutenant Richard Derby of the Fifteenth Massachusetts. *Collection of Ken Fleming.*

Captain Richard C. Derby of the Fifteenth Massachusetts also recalled the mad flight:

> *I went through the whole of* [the battle] *without a scratch, not even a hole in my clothes. I was very disappointed, as some officers had three or four bullets through their coats and caps so I made up for it by nearly drowning myself in the Potomac. I hadn't a suspicion but what I could swim across with ease, so I pulled off my boots, and laid my sword, pistol, and belt on a small board to push across. I was anxious to save my sword, as it looked too much like surrendering to lose that. I kept all my clothes on and my pockets full. I pushed off quite deliberately although the water was full of drowning soldiers and bullets from the rebels on the top of the bluff. I made slow progress with one hand, and had to abandon my raft and cargo. I got along very well a little more than half way, when I found that every effort I made only pushed my head under water, and it suddenly flashed across me that I should drown. I didn't feel any pain or exhaustion—the sensation was exactly like being overcome with drowsiness. I swallowed water in spite of all I could do, till at last I sank unconscious.*[138]

Captain Derby was carried by the Potomac's flow to the shoreline of Harrison's Island, where he was revived by Colonel Devens and carried to an army field hospital.

Captain Henry Tremlett, of Company A of the Twentieth Massachusetts also described the scene in a letter written after the battle:

> *The river was at this time full of swimming and drowning men—a dozen would go below the surface at the same time calling for help. The bullets falling on the river were so thick that the stream resembled a sheet of water during a heavy shower. For my part I expected to be hit every moment and would have been perfectly satisfied to have sent home a few kind words to you that I preferred dying on the field to deserting my men.*[139]

Sergeant Walter A. Eames of the Fifteenth Massachusetts Infantry shared Tremlett's view of escape versus surrender. In a letter to his wife written the day after the battle, Eames noted that he and his Company B comrades were able to escape

> *by swimming the river with the bullets falling like rain all around us. Many were shot and killed in the water. The orders were given for every man to take*

> *care of himself. I saw Col. Devens and Major Kimball preparing to swim so I stripped off all my clothing except my shirt, drawers, and socks and with Colonel Devens, Lt.* [Charles H.] *Eager, Fred Sibley, A.A. Simonds, and George S. Ross, we took some branches off trees for a partial support and struck out for the opposite shore which we succeeded in reaching…Oh didn't the bullets sing merrily around our heads in the passage. The only thing I saved was your picture in the locket. Tell Mr. Thompson that the big pipe is in the Potomac. We threw our arms and equipments* [sic] *into the river to prevent their being service to the enemy. The Colonel and the Major threw their swords as far as they could into the river. I pointed the bayonet into the mud and drive the piece down almost to the lock, leaving it as a mark to start from that next time I travel into Virginia.*[140]

Lieutenant Charles H. Eager, also of the Fifteenth Massachusetts Infantry, remembered the assistance rendered by Private Eames in a letter to his wife:

> *4 of Co. B's boys, A.A. Simonds, Fred Sibley, Walter Eames & Geo. L. Boss insisted on bringing me across the river as they knew I could not swim. So when they began to talk of surrendering I concluded to take the chance, and just as we were about to embark, Col. Devens came along and insisted upon bringing him too, and after a hard struggle we landed safe but just about exhausted. Col. D*[evens] *as well as myself owe our escape to those brave fellows.*[141]

Waiting in reserve on Harrison's Island, the men of the Nineteenth Massachusetts watched the horror unfolding atop the bluff. The regimental historian wrote:

> *The regiment marched in line across the island at sunset, just in time to see the worsted Union forces, hotly pursued, flying in disorder down the opposite bank." He added: "The scene of carnage there witnessed cannot adequately be described….The exultant cries of the foe rose above all the other uproar of battle as the Union men were pushed back to the brink of the bluff and nothing remained, apparently, but surrender or merciless slaughter.*[142]

Not all the Union soldiers abandoned the fight, however. On both ends of the Union line, small detachments of Union soldiers fought on desperately. Captains William Bartlett of the Twentieth Massachusetts and the Irish-born Timothy O'Meara, who had just recently arrived on the Virginia shore with a company of the Tammany Regiment, exhibited remarkable coolness and bravery in leading some of their men back up the bluff for one last skirmish in order to try to buy time for the troops struggling to get over to Harrison's Island. Captain Michael Garetty of Company K of the Tammany Regiment also fought heroically. A New York newspaper report authored by a Tammany soldier vividly described how Garetty grabbed the musket of a fallen enlisted man, took position behind a tree and "with an aim as cool and deliberate as if firing at a target at home, made a number of Secessionists 'bite the dust.'" The soldier claimed that Garetty fell "when three or four shots were directed at him" after his ambush place was discovered and "so enraged were the Rebels at the havoc he had created in their ranks, that [after he died] they visited their vengeance on his inanimate corpse. A cavalry man rode up and with a blow from his sword nearly severed his head from his body."[143]

Captain William F. Bartlett, Twentieth Massachusetts Infantry. *Library of Congress.*

Captain Bartlett was leading his small detachment of men forward from the wood line on the eastern edge of the cleared field when he encountered two companies of the Eighth Virginia (aided by detached companies from the Seventeenth and Eighteenth Mississippi Regiments) emerging from woods on the western end of the field. Bartlett wrote that

> *both sides were so surprised at seeing each other—they at seeing us coming up with this handful of men, we at seeing these two companies drawn up in perfect order—that each side forgot to fire. And we stood looking at each other (not a gun being fired) for some twenty seconds, and then they let fly their volley at the same time we did. If bullets had rained before, they came in sheets now. It is surprising that anyone could escape being hit. We were driven back again.*[144]

In this final fight on the bluff, the twenty-two-year-old flag bearer of the Eighth Virginia, Sergeant T. Clinton Hatcher, was mortally wounded,

Sword presented to Major Paul Revere by his Harvard classmates. *James D. Julia Inc.*

shot through the chest, while spearheading the advance against Bartlett's detachment. The story has been oft-told that many years after the war, when some veterans of the Twentieth Massachusetts visited the battlefield in 1900 and recalled Hatcher's sacrifice, they donated a monument cut of Massachusetts granite to his memory. The monument placed in honor of Hatcher's heroism at Ball's Bluff serves as both a tribute to the brave soldier and as a symbol of a nation reunited.[145]

Following their repulse, Captain Bartlett and his men made their way upriver to the Smart's Mill Ford. Recovering a skiff from the shallow river bottom, Bartlett succeeded in getting the entire group across, five men at a time, to the safety of Harrison's Island.[146] Bartlett recalled that he "ordered those of the regiment that could not swim to follow up the river." He estimated that

> *about 20 of the Twentieth, 20 of the Fifteenth, and 40 of the Tammany and California regiments followed us* [and] *went up as far as the old mill, where* [he] *found, by means of a Negro there, a small sunken skiff in the millway, and induced him to get it out of water and down to the river. It was capable of holding 5 men….In an hour we were all across.*

Captain Tremlett assisted Bartlett in the crossings: "Bartlett and myself had made up our minds to see the men safe across before going ourselves. [Lieutenant] George [Macy] was very loth [*sic*] to go indeed, preferring to remain with me. About 9½ pm we all got across and shall not very soon forget my moonlight paddle across the Potomac.[147]

Colonel Cogswell accepted that the battle was lost and ordered Devens to retreat. Initially, Devens, ever the careful lawyer, refused to accept Cogswell's verbal order unless it was repeated in front of a witness. A newspaper account of the battle written by the war correspondent Charles Carleton Coffin published in the *Boston Journal* on October 26, 1861, claimed that when Colonel Cogswell ordered the final retreat, Colonel Devens replied: "Sir,

I do not wish to retreat. Do you issue it as an order?" Cogswell responded, "Yes," to which Devens requested that the order then "be repeated in the presence of my major [John Kimball]." Cogswell was said to have replied: "I order you to retreat."[148] The *Boston Journal* account is interesting and defensive of the role of a local unit in the battle. Not long before Cogswell's order to retreat, and just after Baker had been killed, Colonel Devens seemed willing to support Colonel Lee's discussion to retreat from the field without argument. It would seem that within just days of the battle, blame for the disaster was already being publically assigned. What is clear, however, is that when word of Cogswell's order was shared as the Union troops tumbled down the banks toward the Potomac, it spread like wildfire in the Union ranks. Soon the entire Union line was crashing down the bluff toward the river in panic.

While small pockets of men continued to engage the enemy up on the bluff or in the woods along the cart path leading down to the river, Colonels Devens and Cogswell independently tried to set up more organized skirmish lines. Finally, recognizing that it was now every man for himself, Devens ordered his men to throw their weapons into the river and try to swim for Harrison's Island.

Colonel Lee was in a similar position. Helped down to the riverbank by some of his men, Lee and a grievously wounded Major Paul Revere, along with some other officers and soldiers, tried to escape upriver. The group attempted to construct a raft by tying fence rails together with their leather sword belts, but the raft soon sank to the river bottom. They continued to make their way upstream until captured by some Confederates from Jenifer's cavalry.[149]

Adjutant Charles Peirson remembered the scene in 1913:

> *Colonel Lee…was a man over middle age, therefore much beyond the rest of us in years, and could not swim the river. He was urged to go in one of the boats, but refused to do so while a single wounded man remained on the Virginia shore. Therefore, some of us whose duty, as we saw it, lay in that direction, accompanied him up the river, hoping if unmolested to reach some Union forces in that quarter. Finding after a while a boat, for which we gave a colored man our only ten dollar gold piece, we endeavored to use it, but a hole in the bottom of it seemed, in the presence of hostile bullets, to make it undesirable, so we proceeded along the bank to a more secure position, where we made a raft of fence rails bound together with our sword belts. It was successfully launched, but before we could use it we were dismayed to see it slowly disappear to rest on the bottom of the river.*[150]

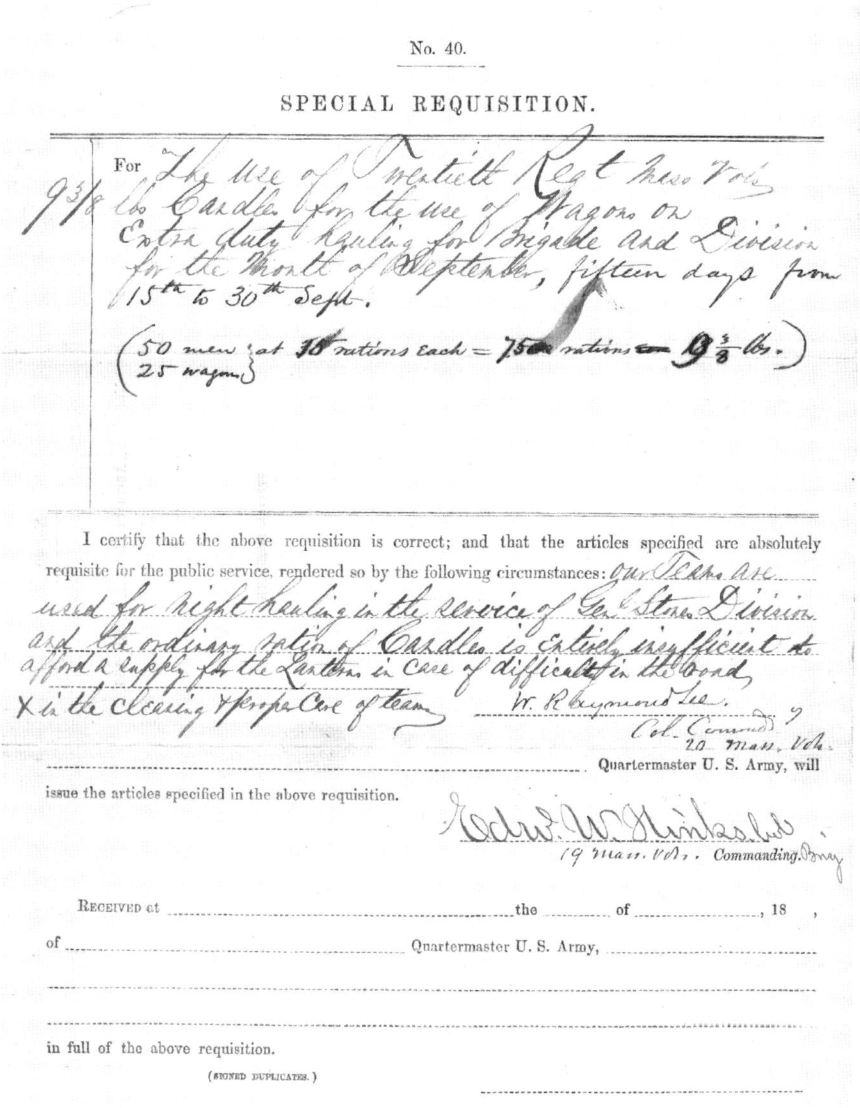

No. 40.

SPECIAL REQUISITION.

For The use of Twentieth Regt Mass Vols
9 3/8 lbs Candles for the use of Wagons on Extra duty hauling for Brigade and Division for the Month of September, fifteen days from 15th to 30th Sept.

(50 men / 25 wagons } at 15 rations each = 750 rations = 9 3/8 lbs.)

I certify that the above requisition is correct; and that the articles specified are absolutely requisite for the public service, rendered so by the following circumstances: Our Teams are used for night hauling in the service of Genl Stone's Division and the ordinary ration of Candles is entirely insufficient to afford a supply for the Lanterns in case of difficulty in the road & in the cleaning & proper care of team

W. Raymond Lee.
Col. Commdg
20 Mass. Vols.

Quartermaster U. S. Army, will issue the articles specified in the above requisition.

Edw. W. Hinks Col
19 Mass. Vols. Commanding Brig

Received at ______ the ______ of ______, 18 ,

of ______ Quartermaster U. S. Army, ______

in full of the above requisition.

(signed duplicates.)

Requisition document signed by Colonel Lee of the Twentieth Massachusetts. *Author's collection.*

Lieutenant Reinhold Wesselhoeft, Company C, Twentieth Massachusetts. *Collection of Ken Fleming.*

Two German-born officers in Company C of the Twentieth Massachusetts, Captain Alois Babo and Lieutenant Reinhold Wesselhoeft, decided to try to avoid capture by swimming across the Potomac. The two had become good friends and plunged into the river together. The regimental history published after the war describes their failed effort to flee:

> *Captains Babo and Lieutenant Wesselhoeft undertook to swim the river without taking off their uniforms, their shoes, or their equipments, even pistols. Nevertheless they seemed to be doing well until, immediately after a volley was fired, one of them was heard to exclaim in German that he was shot, and that was the last that was seen of either of them until Lieutenant Wesselhoeft's body was discovered thirteen days afterwards in the river twenty miles below. As there was no wound upon it, it is probable that Captain Babo was the one shot, and his devoted friend had lost his life in trying to save him.*

Captain Babo's remains were never found.[151]

A Tammany soldier, Private Daniel Ferry of Company A, hid among some battlefield corpses as the Confederates advanced. A newspaper account published under the moniker "Sparks from the Tammany Camp Fires" reported that "while still occupying the recumbent position among the slain, two or three Rebel marauders came along, rifled his pockets of some $20, and cut the buttons from his coat." One of the Confederates proposed stabbing the supposed corpse with his bayonet but was dissuaded by the others, who thought him already dead. "After they were gone," the account continued, "Ferry made tracks for the river." Some Confederates fired upon him as he was trying to swim across the river, but he was able to make it safely to Harrison's Island with just a slight buckshot wound to his back.[152]

Captain John Chandler Putnam of the Twentieth Massachusetts Infantry. *Collection of Ken Fleming.*

In all the confusion, no one seems to have taken note of how many boats were present, but it is likely that only two skiffs, the twenty-five-foot flatboat, a small scow and a metallic lifeboat were available. Some officers tried to reserve the boats for the wounded, but the panicked soldiers piled in and overloaded them. One boat carrying almost one hundred soldiers (many of them wounded) traveled only fifteen or twenty feet into the river before it capsized. Only one man was reported to have survived.[153] From atop the bluff, the Confederates made the escape even more difficult by lining the crest of the bluff and firing down into the river below. Many of the Union soldiers trying to swim to safety were hit by fire coming from the bluff. The Confederates maintained their fire until, as one Southerner recalled, "darkness shut in the bloody work and night in mercy drew her sable curtain over the dead."[154]

The special correspondent for a New York weekly, *The World*, also waxed poetic about the night after the battle:

> *The very skies were pitiless that evening. Oh the misery of the black, tempestuous night, when the rain poured down upon that narrow island where those who escaped the flood and field were bivouacked huddled together, bereft of comrades-in-arms! Scores of the dead were guarded by*

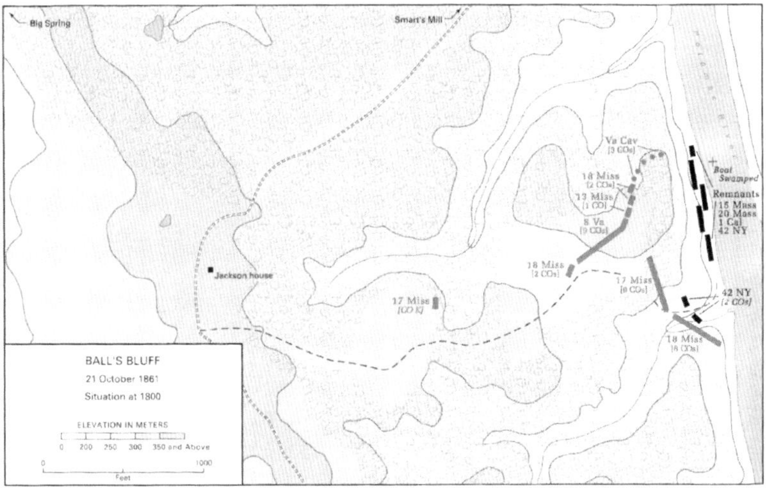

Situation at Ball's Bluff (6:00 p.m.), October 21, 1861. *Center for Military History.*

> *sullen watchers; the wounded were tended in every possible shelter; the river swelled in a kind of savage triumph over the havoc it had made, its current darkling and murmuring on the east and west; while high on that fatal opposite steep lay those whose occupancy even traitors could not then forbid, with pale faces upturned to the darkness of the heavens.*[155]

It was an uneasy night for the Union troops still holding their lines on Harrison's Island. A veteran of the Nineteenth Massachusetts Infantry posted there recalled:

> *It was a terrible night for those on picket. The wounded on the Virginia side of the river cut off from all help could plainly be heard crying for water and begging that a boat be sent over to them. Now and then one could be heard as he waded out into the water, and with strong and steady strokes, breasted the current. Little by little his strokes became weaker, then less steady, then more splashes, in the frantic endeavor to hold out. Then a gurgling sound, a cry for help, and all was still again. All this passed under the senses of willing comrades, powerless to give aid. Now and then, one who was more successful would creep, cold, benumbed and almost dead, up the bank.*[156]

If there was great panic and calamity in the retreat, there also were examples of exceptional heroism and bravery. As the Union soldiers floundered in the Potomac, their comrades on Harrison's Island tried to improvise rafts of whatever material was available. These rafts were then set adrift in hopes they might aid those struggling to make it across. Captain Timothy O'Meara of the Tammany Regiment swam over to Harrison's Island in search of a boat and then swam back over to the Virginia side after he was unable to locate one. Once he reached the safety of Harrison's Island, the captain could have saved himself. Instead, Captain O'Meara believed it was his duty to be with his men. After returning to the Virginia side, he was captured along with many of the men gathered there who were wounded or couldn't make it across. At least one Confederate, Elijah V. White, believed O'Meara deserved the Medal of Honor for his unselfish actions. There would be no Medal of Honor for O'Meara. Just a year later, when O'Meara was serving as the colonel of the Ninetieth Illinois Infantry, he was mortally wounded during the assault on Missionary Ridge in Tennessee. He died on November 26, 1863, and his body was returned to New York, where he was buried in the family plot at the Old Cavalry Cemetery in Queens.[157]

The Nineteenth Massachusetts Infantry maintained its position on Harrison's Island. Colonel Edward Hincks, who commanded the regiment, had arrived there about 1:30 p.m. and struggled to bring order to the transportation problem all through the afternoon. Now, as the Union troops were routed and finding their way back to the island, Hincks formed a defensive line with his regiment, a single cannon from the Rhode Island battery, as well as some men from the Twentieth Massachusetts and the survivors of the Tammany Regiment on Harrison's Island.

On the following morning (October 22), Hincks dispatched Lieutenant Dodge of his regiment over to the Virginia side under a flag of truce, proposing that he be allowed to remove the Union wounded. This request was denied by the Confederates, who permitted only those who were mortally wounded to be evacuated. Permission to allow a Union surgeon to treat the wounded on the Virginia side was also refused, except Colonel Hincks wrote upon the condition that the surgeon should "remain a prisoner in their hands." Later, Colonel Hincks sent Captain Vaughan of the Rhode Island battery over under a separate flag of truce for the purposes of burying the Federal dead, stipulating that "no movement of troops should be made from the island to the Maryland shore in retreat while the burying of the party was employed."[158] Captain Vaughan and the party under his command were able to bury the remains of forty-seven Union soldiers (out of about seventy visible on the field) before dark.

Colonel Edward Hincks of the Nineteenth Massachusetts and his wife. *Library of Congress.*

A controversy arose late in the afternoon of the truce when the Confederate commander charged that Colonel Hincks had violated the provisions of their agreement and threatened to hold Captain Vaughan and his men as prisoners. Colonel Hincks immediately sent over a note clarifying the situation that seemed to satisfy the Confederate officer. Captain Vaughan's party returned after dark, seemingly bringing an end to a long and frustrating day. Colonel Hincks, however, was not so willing to let the situation rest. In his official report of his regiment's participation at Ball's Bluff dated October 23, 1861, Hincks attacked the integrity of the Tammany Regiment and charged that the regiment "deserted [their] post in the intrenchments on the Island at an early hour in the forenoon of the 22d, and passed to the Maryland shore, in disobedience of orders, while I was engaged in arranging for the removal of the wounded and of the burial of the dead."[159]

In early November, General Stone entered the fray and issued Special Order No. 24, firing a withering rebuke at Colonel Hincks. In this order, Stone wrote:

> *The general commanding has, with deep regret, observed in a report by Colonel E.W. Hincks...a statement reflecting severely on the conduct of the gallant Tammany regiment. Colonel Hincks reports that a portion of the Tammany regiment deserted the island....The commanding general deems it proper to give publicity to the fact that he himself requested Major General Banks to relieve the companies of the Tammany regiment early on that morning...Commanding officers are cautioned against making unnecessary and rash statements in their reports, especially in cases where the honor and reputation of other regiments may be involved.*[160]

Undeterred, Colonel Hincks responded to Stone's order by restating the charges against the Tammany Regiment. Hincks requested a formal court of inquiry to counter Stone's censure. In making his case, Hincks argued, for the first time, that because of the cowardly action of the Tammany men on Harrison's Island, gallant men such as Colonel Cogswell and Captain O'Meara were languishing in a Richmond prison because they could not be rescued. The controversy nearly resulted in a duel between Colonel Hincks and an officer from the Tammany Regiment, but no shots (other than those printed in ink) were ever fired. The controversy was never fully resolved. Thirty-two years after the war, in the pages of the veterans' newspaper *National Tribune*, the controversy still raged with charges and countercharges lobbed between the old men of the Massachusetts and Tammany units. Given the passage of history, the entire issue seems founded on a misunderstanding in the wake of the confused battle. The 2d Massachusetts Infantry, a regiment that had been held in reserve during the battle, responded to General Stone's order to General Banks relieve the Tammany men on Harrison's Island, and it appears that the Tammany men simply left their line upon hearing they had been relieved. The Tammany men had little formal command structure on Harrison's Island. It had already been "every man for himself" to even reach the safety of the island and five Tammany officers were absent due to capture. Even Colonel Hincks wrote in his report that he had "so much of the Tammany regiment as was upon the island and could be induced to remain."[161]

In total, the Confederates captured more than 600 prisoners, including Colonels Cogswell of the Tammany Regiment and Colonel Lee and Major Paul Revere of the Twentieth Massachusetts. Despite being wounded in the hand, Colonel Devens was able to swim over to Harrison's Island with the help of another officer from his regiment. The battle's casualties, compared to later engagements, were relatively light, but at the time, they seemed nothing short of disastrous. Of the 1,720 Union soldiers engaged at Ball's Bluff, 127 were killed, 173 wounded and 615 taken prisoner or reported missing.[162] The Confederate casualties at Ball's Bluff were relatively light and reflected the nature of the fight. The Confederates were generally given the advantage of firing from the protection of the woods or from elevated positions. While the Confederates did advance against the Union lines, the Union troops fell back upon being pressed and did not return fire from a fixed defensive position for any significant length of time. Most of the Union fatalities were incurred during the retreat across the river and not on the forward battle line. Of the 1,709 Confederates engaged, 36 were reported killed, 117 were wounded and 3 captured.[163]

After the battle, the Union prisoners were marched into Leesburg, where the officers were questioned by Colonel Evans. Lieutenant William C. Harris of the California Regiment wrote in 1862:

> *The majority of the officers were taken at dusk, and immediately marched under guard to Leesburg…arriving there, the usual rejoicing of an elated and frantic town were performed around us, the towns-people appearing perfectly maddened in their yells of ecstasy and derision, crowding and shouldering each other in herds to catch a glimpse of us. "We've got 'em this time!" "Oh you infernal Yankees!"…were cries that greeted us on every side and it was not until we were marched into the presence of General* [sic] *Evans, the Rebel commander of Leesburg, that the wild uproar of the furious multitude became comparatively silenced.*[164]

Left: Lieutenant Colonel Francis Palfrey of the Twentieth Massachusetts Infantry; *Right*: Captain Charles Peirson of the Twentieth Massachusetts Infantry. *Author's collection.*

Evans offered the Union officers the freedom of the town if they would sign an oath promising not take up arms against the Confederacy until properly exchanged. All of the officers refused the offer and responded that they believed they would be liberated by victorious Union forces later that night. In response, Colonel Evans ordered that the prisoners be taken to the old Manassas battlefield. The prisoners were billeted overnight at the Stone House and from there conveyed to Manassas Junction, where they were put on a train for Richmond.

Adjutant Peirson of the Twentieth Massachusetts remembered:

> *We passed through the battlefield of Bull Run, and halting there were shown into a stone structure* [the Robinson House] *which had been the target for many cannon balls from both sides during the battle. Here was given about midnight a meal, the first in 24 hours, which we managed to slightly cook by making fires upon the floor with laths wrenched from the ceiling. Somewhat refreshed we took passage in open freight cars for Richmond and Libby Prison.*[165]

Captured at Ball's Bluff, Corporal (later Lieutenant) William Henry Cox of the California Regiment. *Collection of Ken Fleming.*

The story of the Ball's Bluff prisoners is a tale featuring its own great drama. While the officers captured at Ball's Bluff were transported by wagon to Manassas, the enlisted men were forced to march. The more than five hundred prisoners marched the thirty-five miles to Manassas after darkness had brought an end to the fighting. They were given just a small ration of cornbread about the size of man's hand according to one account. It was the first morsel of food that many of the men had eaten in thirty-six hours. The men were marched into yards that were enclosed by board fences and then settled in for the night, sleeping on the ground without blankets. They were provided with a small ration of raw ham for dinner. In the morning, the men were given a small loaf of bread and were then separated into groups of fifty men, boarded on open rail cars and transported to Richmond.

The train carrying the prisoners arrived in Richmond midmorning on October 24. The men were then marched under armed guard to a prison that had been established in the Liggon Tobacco Warehouse, a three-story brick building on the corner of Twenty-Fifth and Main Streets in Richmond. The first floor of the building was allotted to officers, with the enlisted men dispersed on the remaining two floors. There were a total of 525 prisoners, including the 22 officers housed at the prison.[166] On the evening of October 30, the newly incarcerated officers from Ball's Bluff were introduced to the other prisoners of war, whom had formed a society known as the

Richmond Prison Association. An official greeting was offered by Edward Taylor of Cincinnati to Colonel Raymond Lee and his officers, who all stood during the address. A prisoner, William H. Jeffrey, who attended the ceremony wrote: "Colonel Lee replied in a dignified and handsome manner, and alluded to the cordial greeting and friendship with which he and his associates had been received since their arrival." Jeffrey added that "Colonel Milton Cogswell and the officers of his command next arose and were introduced by Chaplain Mines of the 2nd Maine Regiment" and that "the Colonel replied with eloquence and grace."[167]

However warm the reception from fellow prisoners, if imprisonment was not enough to concern the Union soldiers captured at Ball's Bluff, the genuine threat of execution soon exacerbated their tension. Back in June 1861, the schooner *Savannah*, operating under orders signed by Confederate president Jefferson Davis and fitted as a privateer, captured a U.S. cargo ship. The *Savannah* was, in turn, captured by a U.S. Navy warship and the crew of the *Savannah* brought to New York City for trial as pirates. Since the United States did not recognize the Confederate government, the "Letters of Marque and Reprisal" signed by President Davis were rejected. The trial of the *Savannah*'s crew was scheduled to begin on October 23, 1861, just two days after the Ball's Bluff battle. This trial concluded without decision eight days later. While all of this was playing out in New York, there was more drama on the high seas that would impact the Ball's Bluff prisoners anxiously waiting for their exchange and release in Richmond.

In late July 1861, the U.S. Navy recaptured the schooner *Enchantress*. This ship had been taken by Confederate privateers and was operating under the command of Captain Walter W. Smith. Smith was attempting to get the ship into a Confederate port as quickly as possible when he and his small crew were captured. Smith was brought to Philadelphia and, after a five-day trial, was ordered to be executed as a pirate. Smith was not immediately executed. This was most likely due to the situation back in New York concerning the issues surrounding the crew of the *Savannah*. Smith was a condemned man, however, and the Confederate authorities were paying attention. After the trial of the *Savannah* crewmen, Confederate officials issued an order demanding a selection of fourteen hostages to be made with the fate of such hostages linked to the fates of Smith and the *Savannah*'s crew.[168]

The selection from the Union prisoners then being held in Richmond was made under the supervision of Confederate general John H. Winder.[169] As detailed in a Confederate War Department communication dated November 9, 1861, Winder reported that

> *one prisoner of the highest rank in our possession was chosen by lot for execution in the same manner as may be adopted by the enemy for the execution of* [Walter W.] *Smith.... The names of the six colonels were placed in a can. The first name drawn, was that of Col.* [Michael] *Corcoran, Sixty-ninth Regiment New York State Militia, who is the hostage chosen to answer for Smith. In choosing the* [remaining] *thirteen from the highest rank to be held to answer for a like number of prisoners of war captured by the enemy at sea, there being only ten field officers it was necessary to draw by lot three captains. The first names drawn were Capts. J*[ames] *B. Ricketts, H*[ugh] *McQuaide and G*[eorge] *W. Rockwood. The list of thirteen will therefore stand—Colonels* [William Raymond] *Lee,* [Milton H.] *Cogswell,* [Orlando B.] *Willcox,* [William] *Woodruff and* [Alfred] *Wood: Lieutenant Colonels* [Henry] *Bowman and* [George] *Neff; Majors* [James] *Potter,* [Paul] *Revere and* [Israel] *Vodges.*

Of these unfortunates, four had been captured at Ball's Bluff. Since Captains Ricketts and McQuaide were suffering from wounds received in battle, their names were replaced by two others drawn by lot, Captain Bowman of the Fifteenth Massachusetts and Captain Francis Keiffer of the First California Regiment, both of whom had been captured at Ball's Bluff. All of the officers selected, with the exception of Colonel Corcoran, were transferred from the tobacco warehouse to the Henrico County Jail. Colonels Cogswell, Lee and Wood, along with Lieutenant Colonel Bowman, Major Revere and Captains Keiffer and Rockwood, were all housed in a single eleven-by-seventeen-foot cell in the jail.[170]

The disposition of the Union and Confederate prisoners was never about legalities. The fate of the prisoners, like the legacy of the Battle of Ball's Bluff itself, always had more to do with the politics than substance. After months of behind-the-scenes negotiations, in February 1862, all of the men tried for piracy were deemed to be prisoners of war and the threat of execution removed. In addition, an agreement was reached providing for an exchange of prisoners between the United States and Confederate governments. In mid-February, about eight hundred Union prisoners were released and sent north by steamer. A like number of Confederates held in Federal camps were exchanged and sent south. Included in the number of Union soldiers liberated were all of the Ball's Bluff prisoners held in Richmond, with the exception of Captain Timothy O'Meara. Unfortunately for Captain O'Meara, who had demonstrated great heroism at Ball's Bluff, he had been transferred from Richmond to a Confederate prison in Alabama and was not included in the exchange reached between the Union and Confederate negotiators. It was not until August 1862 that Captain O'Meara was paroled and liberated from his incarceration. Also released at this time was Colonel Corcoran. The friendship that developed between Corcoran and O'Meara during their imprisonment resulted in Corcoran recommending O'Meara's promotion to command a new Irish regiment that was being organized in Chicago.

6

Someone Had Blundered

General Stone did not receive the first reports of the bad news from the battlefield until about 6:30 p.m. At 6:45 p.m. he telegraphed McClellan, reporting, "Colonel Baker has been killed at the head of his brigade. I [will] go to the right at once." President Lincoln was visiting McClellan's headquarters when the message was received, and an army lieutenant escorted the president into an inner office to break the news to him. Lincoln reportedly staggered out of the office, his hands pressed hard against his chest; he stumbled when he stepped out into the street (McClellan feared he would fall) and returned to the White House without a word to anyone. To Lincoln, Baker was an old and trusted friend, and his death hit hard. Lincoln's private secretary, John Hay, recalled that as the president and his commanders gathered at McClellan's headquarters to consider the news of Baker's death:

> *A king might have been proud of the simple and hearty eulogies uttered last night in McClellan's room, where the President, and Seward, and Cameron and M'Clellan, and another, in deep but not unmanly grief, received the heavy news of their friend. Each had his word of earnest sorrow and honest praise. The President mourned the sundering of the dearest of those ties that connected him with the memory of a happier and more careless day.*[171]

After he returned to the White House, President Lincoln told his wife, Mary, and his sons about Baker's death and then retired to his office, where he remained for the rest of the evening.

Brigadier General Charles P. Stone. *Author's collection.*

On the day before the battle, Lincoln and Baker had sat and shared a picnic on the White House lawn. It had been a beautiful fall day, and while Lincoln's son Willie played in the leaves nearby, the two old friends shared their thoughts about the war. Baker spoke of the progress of the war. He was anxious to secure promotion to higher rank. As he rose to leave, Willie ran to him. Baker picked him up and kissed the boy, remarking that he had known Willie since he was a baby. John Hay remembered that Baker had come down to Washington to organize his affairs (and likely lobby for a major general's commission). As Baker and President Lincoln talked warmly, Mary Lincoln came out and presented Baker with a bouquet of flowers. Hay recalled that Baker thanked the First Lady for her kindness and responded, "Very beautiful, these flowers and my memory will wither together."[172] After a while, Baker mounted his horse and rode out of the White House gates; Lincoln watched after him until he disappeared from view.[173]

Now he was gone, killed within forty miles of the Capitol in a battle that had gone terribly wrong. Lincoln paced his office all night long, while the rain pelted at the windows; in another room of the White House, Willie Lincoln wrote a poem in honor of the family's fallen friend. The poem later appeared in the Washington paper *National Republican*. The paper's readers might have marveled that such a composition could be authored by a ten-year-old boy:

There was no patriot like Baker,
So noble and so true;
He fell as a soldier on the field,
His face to the sky of blue….

No squeamish notions filled his breast,
The Union was his theme,
"No surrender and no compromise,"
His day thought and night's dream.

His country has her part to play,
To'rds those he left behind
His widow and his children all—
She must always keep in mind.[174]

While Lincoln mourned the loss of his friend and McClellan tried to learn more details about the situation at Ball's Bluff, back at Edward's Ferry, it was a difficult night for General Stone. His force was in a shambles; each fragmentary bit of additional information he gained from the Union officers and men on Harrison's Island seemed to paint a progressively darker picture of what had taken place on the bluff. At 9:45 p.m., he broke the bleak news to McClellan: "I deeply regret to report a repulse on the right after Colonel Baker's death. I have called on General Banks for more troops. The enemy were re-enforced at the time of confusion, and our loss is severe. We still hold Harrison's Island." McClellan replied, still not fully grasping the extent of the repulse: "Hold your position on the Virginia side of the Potomac at all hazards. General Banks will support you with one Brigade at Harrison's Island and the other at Seneca. [Brigadier General Frederick W.] Lander will be with you at daylight." It was support that would come too late.[175]

The Confederates, however, weary from the fight and low on ammunition, showed no signs of following up on their victory. Indeed, as night fell, the Mississippi regiments moved back from the river and went into camp in an open field just outside of Leesburg. Only two companies, under Lieutenant Colonel McGuirk, were left behind to stand guard. Colonel Hunton ordered the Eighth Virginia to return to Fort Evans, detailing only a small force of twelve men, including Elijah White, to remain on the battlefield as pickets. Later in the evening, while scouting the area at the base of the bluff, these pickets encountered some of the Union survivors of the Tammany Regiment. Shots were exchanged, and the pickets crept back up the bluff. Elijah White rode back to Leesburg to provide details regarding the instability of the Virginia shoreline. Informing Colonel Hunton that there were apparently still large numbers of Union soldiers stranded on the Virginia shore, Hunton ordered Captain William Berkeley and about forty men of the Eighth Virginia to scout the riverbank. Under White's guidance, the Confederates were able to capture a few hundred Union survivors who were unable to get across the river during the frenzied retreat of the main Federal force.[176]

It had been a long and difficult day for the Union army, and this final chapter added insult to the general feeling of despair. The Federals had been

Brigadier General Frederick W. Lander. *Author's collection.*

defeated, and no one took this more personally than General Stone. Stone and his staff officers desperately tried to discover what had gone wrong. To complicate matters, each survivor of the fight seemed to tell a different story of the disaster. The scene on Harrison's Island and the Maryland shore was pandemonium, and it would not be until morning that the remaining officers could restore some semblance of order to the mixed commands. At 10:30 p.m., General Stone sat down at his desk at headquarters and wrote the following report to President Lincoln:

> *It is impossible to give full particulars of what is yet inexplicable to me. Our troops under Col. Baker were reported in good condition and position within 15 minutes of the death of Col. Baker. We have still possession of Harrison's Island and some fifteen hundred men on the Virginia side opposite Edward's Ferry. Six hundred more going over. We have lost several field officers killed and wounded and Colonels Lee and Cogswell are said to be prisoners. Colonel Ward wounded. The enemy has not thus far attempted any attack of our positions. We have lost two mountain howitzers and one Rifled James Gun. The enemy was undoubtedly reinforced in the evening but how much is impossible to say. The report of killed by me an hour before the disaster was 30. Our killed and wounded may reach 200, numbers of prisoners unknown.*[177]

The Union force on the Virginia side opposite Edward's Ferry concerned Stone. Although he had support on its way from General Banks, Stone worried that the Confederate force that had challenged Baker's force would now turn its attention to Gorman's brigade. Early on the morning of October 22, General Banks arrived and assumed command. The two officers discussed the situation. As the last orders received from General McClellan directed Stone to "hold this position," Stone had already sent Gorman additional entrenching tools with instructions to "intrench [*sic*] and hold out against whatever force might appear."[178] It was sound advice, for on the afternoon of October 22, Gorman's troops were attacked by Confederates under the command of Colonel William Barksdale. It was Barksdale's Thirteenth Mississippi that held Gorman's men in check while Colonel Evans directed most of his force into the fight at Ball's Bluff. However, while the Mississippians had largely been kept out of the previous day's fight, they were severely bloodied in the attack on Gorman's troops. Barksdale described the fight in his official report:

> *On Tuesday morning, I was ordered…to reconnoiter the enemy at Edward's Ferry, and attack him if in my judgment his numbers and position would warrant me in doing so. Reaching the ground, I occupied the day before, I ordered Captain Randell to skirmish on my left and Captain Eckford on my right. They reported that the enemy in very large numbers were stationed, as on the preceding day, near the banks of the river. From their movements, which could be easily seen from my position, I supposed they were planting a battery at the point of woods jutting out into the field to the right of the Daily house. I determined to make the attack at that point, and accordingly, ordered Captain Eckford to commence the engagement, and to charge and take the battery, if one should be found there.*
>
> *Taking the road leading to Kephart's Mill, I halted the regiment in the woods to the right of the Daily plantation, and in a few minutes Captain Eckford commenced the attack upon several companies of pickets which were stationed along the field, charging upon and driving them in great disorder and confusion before his fire. I ordered the regiment at once to advance, and the engagement in a moment became general. Under a heavy fire from the enemy's batteries on both sides of the river and an incessant fire from his lines on this side, the regiment continued to advance some 400 yards, firing as it advanced, driving the enemy before it back to the river, and killing, so far as I have been able to learn, 35 or 40 of their number. The enemy having been driven back behind his field works, and greatly outnumbering my command, having also artillery on both sides of the river, I did not deem it proper further to continue the assault, and hence withdrew the regiment to its position near Fort Evans, which I reached after dark.*[179]

This attack by Barksdale's force and the tenuous foothold Gorman's brigade had on the Virginia shore was too reminiscent of Baker's position for Stone's comfort. Fearing a repetition of the Ball's Bluff disaster, Gorman's force was pulled out of Virginia and returned to the Maryland shore during the evening of October 22.[180] As a parting compliment to the Confederates, the remaining guns of the Rhode Island Light Artillery fired a salvo at the Virginia shore after the last Union troops were safely on Maryland soil.[181] While this action ended the military engagement along General Stone's Potomac line, the official effort to assign blame for the disaster was just beginning.

General McClellan apparently thought that he would help clarify the matter when he issued an army circular on October 24, 1861, directed to the divisional commanders of the Army of the Potomac. McClellan had personally gone to Stone's headquarters and listened to the details of the battle as reconstructed by General Stone, and though he seemed satisfied with the general's handling of the operation, he was careful to shift responsibility away from himself. McClellan's circular concluded: "The disaster was caused by errors committed by the immediate Commander [Edward Baker] not General Stone. I have withdrawn all the troops from the other side, since they went there without my orders & nothing was to be gained by retaining them there."[182] McClellan had seen how the Manassas debacle had ripped apart the reputations of the officers in command and was well aware that Washington was a strange city often fueled more by politics than logic. General McClellan recognized in Ball's Bluff the elements of a political problem and quickly moved to protect his reputation. On October 25, McClellan confided to his wife: "That affair at Leesburg on Monday last was a terrible butchery—the men fought nobly but were penned up by a vastly superior force in a place where they had no retreat. The whole thing took place some 40 miles from here without my orders or knowledge—it was entirely unauthorized by me & I am in no manner responsible for it." McClellan continued, "[T]he man directly to blame for the affair was Col Baker who was killed—he was in command, disregarded entirely the instructions he had received from Stone, & violated all military rules & precautions."[183]

As the weeks passed, the bloated bodies of dead soldiers floated down the Potomac. The remains of some were found wedged into the rocks at Great Falls, while others were caught in the stone foundation of the Aqueduct Bridge near Georgetown. Each time a new body was discovered, the Washington newspapers reported the grisly find. With each discovery, the nation was reminded of the tragedy. As winter settled in and the members of Congress returned from their districts to once again fill the Capitol's chambers, it became clear that the final chapter on the Ball's Bluff debacle was not yet written. For some, the full legacy of Ball's Bluff had not even begun to take hold.

7

Congressional Inquiry and the Search for Blame

While the military results of Ball's Bluff were negligible, the political repercussions of the battle were extraordinary given the small-scale nature of the fight.[184] In the weeks after the battle, a vigorous public debate filled the newspapers with opinions as to who was responsible for the disaster. Supporters of General Stone, a loyal cadre of regular army officers, leveled harsh criticism at Colonel Baker, while Baker's friends and admirers, not a few at the highest levels of the government, blamed Stone and were vocal in calling for a formal court of inquiry. The litany of charges and countercharges soon devolved into an argument that pitted professional regular army officers against those in the volunteer force. Each side utilized examples culled from the tragic chronology of the battle to its advantage. The regular army officers suggested that nothing short of disaster could be expected when volunteers were entrusted with the responsibility to command important operations, while the volunteers countered that the professional army command corps was inept, creating debacles like First Manassas/Bull Run and Ball's Bluff through incompetent military administration.

The U.S. Congress was not immune from the public discourse. Out of session since the summer, members of the House and Senate had endured one military disaster after another. Congress supported President Lincoln's role as commander in chief but also urged action. In advocating a more aggressive war policy, Congress grew increasingly frustrated when the Union army under General McClellan repeatedly failed to take the initiative. The members of Congress tried to be patient, but the lack of action reflected poorly on Lincoln's administration and lent credibility to those who suggested that Lincoln might not be up to the challenge of a wartime presidency. There was a growing movement among some in Congress to set a course that would force military action. As the historian Bruce Tap has observed, "given the Whig antecedents in the Republican party, there was nothing particularly unique about the legislative branch attempting to influence the executive."[185] It was common thought at the time that despite the president's role as commander in chief, Congress should play a major role in shaping and directing military policy.[186]

Senator Benjamin Wade. *Author's collection.*

It was amid this atmosphere that the Second Session of the Thirty-Seventh United States Congress opened on December 2, 1861. Action began in the Senate on December 5, 1861, when Ohio Republican senator Benjamin F. Wade introduced a resolution calling for the formation of a committee of three, with authority to subpoena individuals and papers associated with the "disasters" at Bull Run and Ball's Bluff. Wade's motion unleashed a floodgate of proposals, with other senators offering amendments authorizing the committee to investigate other military calamities, including those of Wilson's Creek and Lexington, both Union defeats in Missouri, as well as the Belmont, Missouri, and Big Bethel, Virginia battles. In the wake of this clamor, Senator Zachariah Chandler withdrew his resolution, a move that helped to maintain lively congressional discussion about the Ball's Bluff debacle and inspired Senator James W. Grimes of Iowa to introduce a resolution establishing a committee with an even broader investigatory scope.[187] The resolution specified that a joint committee of three senators and four members of the House of Representatives "be appointed to inquire into the conduct of the present war, and that they have the power to send for persons and papers, and to sit during the sessions of either House of Congress." The Grimes Resolution extended the power of the committee to investigate not only disasters of the past but also the conduct of the war in general.

While some members of the Senate protested that the committee's authority was too broad, the resolution passed the Senate on December 9, 1861, by a vote of thirty-three to three. Senator Lafayette S. Foster of Connecticut was one of the few to voice dissent over the resolution, proclaiming: "If it is an inquiry which the military authorities ought to make, and they do not make, I for one…will not vote to make it at the present time." Foster believed in "letting the military authorities manage the Army"; if the war was being ineptly managed, Foster warned, "in heaven's name do not let us make it worse by tampering, for worse we shall make it, and only worse." Despite Foster's rhetoric, he was ultimately persuaded by his colleagues to vote in favor of the resolution.[188]

On December 10, 1861, the House of Representatives unanimously approved the proposal, and the controversial Joint Committee on the Conduct of the War was established. Its Senate members, appointed by Vice President Hannibal Hamlin, were Republican senators Benjamin Wade (Ohio) and Zachariah Chandler (Michigan) and the Unionist Democrat Andrew Johnson (Tennessee). Senator Joseph Wright of Indiana later replaced Johnson. Senator Wade was selected to chair the committee. Both he and Senator Chandler were radical Republicans and staunch opponents of slavery who believed that the war was the engine that would bring an end to the South's "peculiar institution." A Cincinnati newspaper described Wade as a man "rich in epithets and profligate in furious vituperation."[189] After President Lincoln countermanded an order—emancipating slaves in Missouri—by one of his generals back in August 1861, Wade attributed the president's views on race to "one born of poor white trash and educated in a slave state."[190] Intemperate and direct, neither Senator Wade nor Senator Chandler exhibited patience for anything that stood in the way of achieving the goal of winning the war and eliminating slavery. The House members of the committee were the Republicans Daniel W. Gooch (Massachusetts), George W. Julian (Indiana), John Covode (Pennsylvania) and the sole Democrat, Moses F. Odell (New York). From the beginning, the committee was directed by Senators Wade and Chandler and Representatives Julian and Gooch. Under their leadership, the committee used subpoena powers, held closed sessions and arranged a system under which business could be conducted without a quorum. This last maneuver allowed hearings to be conducted, as well as testimony to be taken, when just one committee member—frequently Wade—was present. The powerful Republican senator from Ohio would rule the inquiry with an iron hand.[191]

The committee's formal investigation into the Ball's Bluff disaster began in December 1861, and General McClellan was scheduled to be its first witness. McClellan, however, was too ill to testify, having been stricken with a condition diagnosed by his doctors as typhoid fever. President Lincoln, upon hearing that his commanding general was seriously ill, confided his frustrations to Quartermaster General Montgomery Meigs. With no small amount of desperation, Lincoln asked Meigs for advice, lamenting: "The people are impatient; [Secretary of the Treasury] Chase has no money and he tells me he can raise no more; the General of the Army has typhoid fever. The bottom is out of the tub. What shall I do?" Newspapers began openly discussing the possibilities of McClellan's successor.[192]

On December 27, 1861, the Committee on the Conduct of the War called its first witness. It was Brigadier General Frederick W. Lander, a brigade commander in General Stone's division. Lander, well known as an intrepid western explorer before the war, had been in Washington while the fighting raged at Ball's Bluff. He had resigned his command before the battle to accept a different post, but his resignation had not yet been accepted. He was ordered by General McClellan to go to the front and arrived just in time for the skirmish at Edward's Ferry on October 22. In this brisk action, he had been wounded in the leg. It was only a slight wound, but it continued to trouble him in the months that followed and likely contributed to his death in March 1862.[193] Given the opportunity to testify before the congressional committee, General Lander gave the impression that he was present at Ball's Bluff and was quick to criticize General Stone's actions on the field. In his testimony, Lander suggested that, had he been in command, Leesburg would have easily fallen into Union hands. He claimed that nearly two weeks before the battle, he had laid out a plan to capture Leesburg. His plan, he said, involved moving McCall's troops up the Leesburg Pike and using Banks's force to cross over the Potomac and support McCall. When pressed for his opinion of General Stone, Lander replied that he found Stone to be "an excellent officer" but that he had been "tripped up by circumstances." Lander remarked that Stone was "very efficient and orderly" but had made an inexcusable error in the adequacy of river transport. He expressed his self-confident opinion that his personal experience in western exploration, including many river crossings on the frontier, would have produced better results in the operation had he been in command.[194]

Lander was followed on the witness stand by Brigadier General George A. McCall, whose force had invested Dranesville and who was thought by Stone to have been moving in the direction of Leesburg under McClellan's

Army paymaster Dwight Banister testified against General Stone. *Author's collection.*

orders when Colonel Devens's men were skirmishing near the Bluff. McCall laid his case before the committee, testifying he had performed his duties to the letter, conducted a bloodless advance toward Dranesville and retired, as directed by General McClellan, in total ignorance of Stone's operation. McCall concluded, however, that had he been apprised of Stone's reliance upon his anticipated advance from Dranesville he could have, with some difficulty, captured Colonel Evans and his entire Confederate command.[195]

While the generals testified in secret, defenders of Colonel Baker were initiating a battle of words in the Washington newspapers, trying to shift the blame for the Ball's Bluff debacle onto the already overburdened shoulders of General Stone. Critics claimed that Baker had been ordered across the Potomac by Stone and had been sacrificed as a victim of Stone's incompetence. Orders stained by Baker's blood were referenced to substantiate the claims. These orders, said to have been recovered from the interior band of Baker's hat—and undoubtedly doctored, perhaps by Baker's loyal subaltern Captain Francis Young—were published in the October 27, 1861 *Hartford Weekly Times* and purportedly directed Baker to "make a dash at Leesburg, and shoot down any lawless depredator that may leave the ranks," The "orders" further reported that "Gen. Gorman is moving up on the left" and that Stone expected "to be in possession of Leesburg to-night." An aide to Colonel Baker reported that after receiving the order, Baker had dramatically muttered, "I will obey General Stone's orders, but it is my death warrant."

The committee never reviewed the bloodstained orders. Captain Young claimed to have preserved the document and said he had given them to Assistant Secretary of War Edward D. Townsend. Young said that Townsend had agreed to return the orders but had not done so. Young's claims, like much of his testimony before the committee, are highly questionable. If the War Department was in possession of a document that would have cleared Colonel Baker and substantiated claims against General Stone, the administration clearly would have directed that it be offered into evidence.

Even if the War Department or the Lincoln administration declined to produce such an incriminating document, had the orders existed, the broad jurisdiction of the congressional committee would have authorized the committee to demand that they be produced. No such request was ever made.[196]

General Stone did not react to this criticism of his command publicly, but he composed a private letter to General McClellan in which he denounced the charges of Baker's friends as being "absurd" and reported that "the plain truth is that this brave and impetuous officer was determined to bring on an action, and made use of the discretion allowed him to do it." Stone believed that the responsibility for Ball's Bluff would eventually fall on Baker's shoulders, and in this belief, he demonstrated remarkable political naiveté. The Committee on the Conduct of the War was created with dual purpose of investigating both Union military failures in general and the Ball's Bluff fight in particular. The mission was hardly impartial, as the Ball's Bluff debacle had cost the life of one of Congress's most respected members; those more familiar with the political process than General Stone knew that it would be unprecedented for the committee to find fault with the martyred Baker.

Unaware of the previous testimony provided to Senator Wade, General Stone appeared before the committee on January 5, 1862. Although Stone had read the newspapers and knew that there was public call for those responsible for the disaster to be identified and appropriately punished, he thought that his testimony before the committee would allow him to explain his command decisions and clear his name. There is little doubt from the tenor of Stone's testimony that he fully believed that an informed review of the Ball's Bluff affair would conclude in his favor. He fully cooperated with the committee's investigation with great enthusiasm—little realizing that he was assisting with his own prosecution. Stone was a professional soldier, a man whose life and military career were directed by discipline and obedience to duty. When he stood before Senator Wade's secret panel of interrogators, he was severely overmatched.

If Stone had confidence that his testimony might clear his name, such hopes should have been dashed when the bombastic but influential New York senator Roscoe Conkling took to the floor of the House and unleashed a torrent of accusations against him. Most of these went unanswered, as Stone, a professional military officer and not a politician, had not lined up supporters to engage in a political fight. Stone's cause was further complicated by President Lincoln's move to replace Secretary of War

Secretary of War Edwin Stanton. *Author's collection.*

Simon Cameron with Edwin Stanton. Stanton, an accomplished Cincinnati attorney, antislavery Democrat and McClellan loyalist, had briefly served as President Buchanan's attorney general before joining Lincoln's "team of rivals." He immediately allied himself with the committee to distance the administration and General McClellan from the Ball's Bluff calamity.[197]

During their questioning of General Stone, the members of the congressional committee were careful to obscure the real purpose of their questioning. One historian has described it as "a perfect storm of political intrigue."[198] There was little indication or suggestion that the committee doubted Stone's loyalty or military capabilities, and the inquiry seemed limited to queries about the tactical aspects of the Ball's Bluff fight. The direction of the congressional investigation took a sudden turn, however, on January 10, 1862, when Colonel George Tompkins, commander of the Second New York State Militia, gave his testimony. The only senior officer to directly condemn General Stone, Colonel Tompkins had not even been present at Ball's Bluff but questioned Stone's loyalty to the Union cause. In his testimony, Tompkins alluded to rumors of sealed letters sent across the Potomac under Stone's order and flags of truce arranged so that civilians might pass back and forth through the lines. Tompkins claimed that "there is not a man in my regiment that will fight under him, if they can avoid it" and indicated that a petition was being circulated to have his unit removed from Stone's command. The committee members were deeply affected by Tompkins's testimony, some of which was later repeated by other officers, who told of mysterious packages transported across the Potomac and strange lantern signals observed at night along the Confederate side of the river.[199]

Colonel Tompkins was grinding a sharp axe of retribution in his testimony before the committee. At First Manassas, his regiment had faltered, and Tompkins had been charged with "misbehavior before the enemy" in refusing to follow an order to attack. When General Stone absorbed the regiment into his command following the battle, he had leaned hard on the troubled unit and its appointed officers. Stone had even added a charge of financial irregularities in accounting against Tompkins. Two of Tompkins's fellow officers in the regiment also were charged in the affair. Both of these men were released from military arrest to testify against Stone. In fact, ten of the thirty-six witnesses against Stone were all from the Second New York State Militia. These witnesses each relayed well-rehearsed and hearsay testimony consistent with Colonel Tompkins's undocumented account of Stone's disloyalty and unfitness for command.[200]

The committee accepted Tompkins's testimony despite assurances from Lieutenant Colonel Wistar, who had been on the field at Ball's Bluff, that the army had complete confidence in General Stone. Although he had been a close friend of Baker's, Lieutenant Colonel Wistar refused to criticize Stone and suggested that Colonel Baker, rather than Stone, was probably responsible for the disaster. Having whiffed the tinge of disloyalty, however, the Committee largely ignored Wistar's testimony, and continued to seek out witnesses critical of Stone.[201] Following Wistar's appearance, the members of the committee visited the newly appointed Secretary of War Edwin Stanton to inform him of their suspicions about Stone's loyalty.

Although the committee's prime objective was to investigate the administration of the Ball's Bluff battle, the cabal increasingly turned its attention toward General Stone. While at one point the committee might have been satisfied to find a scapegoat for the Ball's Bluff affair that would merely deflect public criticism away from Colonel Baker, it now shifted its purpose and initiated a full-scale assault on Stone's professional and personal reputation. This turnabout has intrigued many historians who have examined the Ball's Bluff fiasco, and while it may have had much to do with Stone's inability to effectively respond to the charges leveled against him, it is likely that other forces were also at work. In targeting Stone, the committee was trying to impugn General McClellan's administration of the war. A staunch Democrat—who in 1864 would challenge Lincoln for the presidency—McClellan did not push an aggressive military agenda against slavery. McClellan's driving ambition was to restore the Union, not destroy slavery. For the more radicalized politicians who felt otherwise, an attack on Stone was an attack on his immediate superior, Lincoln's handpicked commander, George B. McClellan. General Stone just made the task easier for the committee.

Complicating things further, in the fall of 1861, General Stone had assisted in the return of several fugitive slaves who had entered his lines and taken refuge in the camp of the Twentieth Massachusetts Infantry. In September 1861, Stone had issued an order to his Corps of Observation forbidding any interference with slavery.[202] While the return of these slaves to their owners in Maryland and Virginia was consistent with President Lincoln's established policies, it put Stone at odds with several Massachusetts volunteer officers who were strongly antislavery. Using the same political influence that had gained their military commissions, the New Englanders wrote a letter to the abolitionist governor of Massachusetts, John A. Andrew, denouncing Stone's actions.

Senator Charles Sumner of Massachusetts. *Library of Congress.*

Governor Andrew was swift in responding and forwarded a strongly worded letter to the colonel of the Twentieth Massachusetts encouraging disobedience of Stone's order. When Stone learned of Governor Andrew's attempt to circumvent his military command, he sent off a sharp letter of protest to General McClellan. McClellan understood Stone's complaint and endorsed the letter, but the two commanders gained no friend in Governor Andrew when Stone's letter was made public. Governor Andrew intensified his tirade, asserting that the Massachusetts volunteers were properly subject to his orders and instructed Senator Charles Sumner, a prominent Radical Republican from Massachusetts, to denounce Stone in a speech delivered before the U.S. Senate. Sumner, an abolitionist hero who had famously been assaulted on the floor of the Senate by a proslavery congressman from South Carolina back in 1856, complied with the desires of his governor and unleashed a flurry of accusations against Stone. At one point in his tirade, Sumner accused Stone of "engaging ably and actively in the work of surrendering fugitive slaves."[203] Stone responded by effectively challenging Senator Sumner to a duel, a challenge that President Lincoln thought justified, but one that Sumner wisely ignored. Stone closed his letter of challenge: "There can hardly be better proof that a soldier in the field is faithfully performing his duty, than the fact that while he is receiving the shot of the public enemy in front he is at the same time receiving the vituperation of a well-known coward from a safe distance in the rear."[204]

The exchange was not without a lasting result, however, as both Stone and McClellan struggled to escape a controversy that had generated great animosity from the powerful Radical Republican faction in Congress. The extent of this animosity materialized in ways that General Stone could have scarcely imagined.

8

The Arrest and Imprisonment of General Stone

On January 28, 1862, Secretary of War Edwin Stanton met with General George B. McClellan and presented the details of the government's case against General Stone. Relying on emergency detention powers that Stanton transferred from the Department of State to the War Department, General McClellan was provided with an order calling for Stone's immediate arrest.[205] McClellan was surprised by this turn of events and suggested that Stone should first be permitted to answer the charges posted against him. It was the first, and only time during the entire history of the Ball's Bluff fiasco, that McClellan interceded on Stone's behalf. McClellan convinced Stanton to temporarily suspend the arrest order and urged the secretary to approach Senator Wade, chairman of the congressional committee investigating Ball's Bluff, to schedule a second hearing.

McClellan's suggestion to delay Stone's arrest may not have been so altruistic. Attorney General Edward Bates recalled a meeting between McClellan and Colonel James Van Alen in which McClellan had suggested that the committee needed a victim. Van Alen had replied, "Yes—and when they have once tasted blood, got one victim, no one can tell who will be the next victim!" On hearing this, Bates reported that McClellan "colored up, and the conversation ceased."[206] Although Attorney General Bates professed to know little of the case against Stone, he wrote a confidential note to Secretary of War Stanton advising him to not be hasty in "complying with the demand" for Stone's arrest.[207]

Brigadier General Charles P. Stone and daughter. *Library of Congress.*

On January 31, 1862, just three days after Stanton's meeting with McClellan, and with hardly any time to prepare a formal defense, General Stone was called to testify before the committee.[208]

At no point during this hearing, or indeed afterward, was Stone provided with the names of his accusers or the transcripts of any of the testimony made against him. In relation to the military matters at issue, Stone was disabled by McClellan's broad stipulation that none of the orders from his headquarters relating to the Ball's Bluff operation could be revealed. As McClellan's assistant adjutant general, Lieutenant Colonel Richard B. Irwin, later observed in an article written for the *Century Magazine*, Stone was not even informed of the charges issued against him.[209] Senator Wade implied that on several points, the committee's investigation had uncovered evidence that tended to "impeach" Stone's conduct. Wade indicted that Stone had sent troops to Ball's Bluff without sufficient means of transportation, had failed to reinforce and support the operation appropriately and maintained "undue communication with the enemy by letters that have passed back and forth" and "by intercourse with officers of the other side."[210]

The tenor of Stone's testimony suggests that he still had no idea of the seriousness of the situation. His anger flared only in response to questions regarding his patriotism; reacting to Senator Wade's comment that Stone had maintained inappropriate communications with the enemy, the maligned general retorted:

> *That is one humiliation I had hoped I never should be subjected to. I thought there was one calumny that could not be brought against me. Any other calumny that anybody can raise I should expect, after what I have received; but that one I should have supposed that you, personally, Mr. Chairman, would have rejected at once. You remember last winter when this government had so few friends, who had this city, I might almost say, in his power? I raised all the volunteer troops that were here during the seven dark days of last winter. I disciplined and posted those troops. I commanded them, and I led them. I could have surrendered Washington. And now I will swear that this government has not a more faithful soldier; of poor capacity, it is true; but a more faithful soldier this government has not had from the day General Scott called me, the 31st day of December, 1860, up to this minute.*[211]

Following Stone's testimony, the committee adjourned. On the evening of February 4, 1862, the members of the committee met with Secretary Stanton to review the evidence. Although the details of this meeting remain unknown, it is likely that the members discussed Stone's most recent testimony and its impact on the case they had constructed against him. For his part, Stone seems to have been satisfied that he effectively addressed the committee's concerns. On the evening of February 5, he attended a White House reception at President Lincoln's invitation and, just two nights later, dined with General McClellan at his Washington headquarters. Curiously enough, on the same day Stone dined at McClellan's table, McClellan had submitted a report to Secretary Stanton of grave significance. McClellan claimed that he received information that a refugee who came into the Union lines from Leesburg and whom had been questioned by Union officers indicated "how much the Confederates thought of their friend Stone." McClellan's role in this drama seems uncertain, but his submission of the report regarding the refugee's unconfirmed story to Secretary Stanton and his unwillingness to share details of the report with Stone did little to assist his embattled subaltern. McClellan never provided Stone with the details of the refugee's report and, in the coming weeks, directed a staff officer to respond to Stone's request for more specifics. The staff officer wrote to Stone in early December 1862 to relate that McClellan could no longer recollect the name of the refugee and that the report documenting the circumstances was among his official papers then in transit to New York.

Major General George Sykes. *Author's collection.*

After receiving McClellan's report, Stanton reissued the order for Stone's arrest.[212] General McClellan complied with Stanton's directive and drafted the necessary military orders effecting Stone's arrest. On the evening of February 8, 1862, General Stone was returning to his home from a late-night meeting at Willard's Hotel. As he approached his residence, he observed a military officer waiting for his arrival. He recognized the officer as George Sykes, an old friend from Stone's service in the Fourteenth United States Infantry. Sykes had recently been promoted to the rank of brigadier general and was in charge of Washington's city guard. As General Stone greeted him, he immediately understood that Sykes was there on official business. Sykes commented that he had "disagreeable duty" to perform and that he was there to place Stone under arrest.[213] General Stone was astounded and asked what charges were being proffered against him, but Sykes responded that he did not know and was simply under orders to facilitate the arrest and see that General Stone was transported under armed guard to Fort Lafayette (a prison located in New York Harbor where political prisoners were often interned). Stone was incredulous and raged that "Fort Lafayette was where they send secessionists!," but Sykes could only respond with a muted "Yes."[214] Stone then went inside his home, changed into civilian clothing and returned. It was then that he noticed the armed guard detail that had hidden in the shadows while he and Sykes had discussed the arrest. Stone was escorted down to the Chain Building, the headquarters for the city guard, where he was directed to empty his pockets and surrender his papers. He was quartered in a lieutenant's bedroom for the night with an armed sentry stationed outside.

The next morning, Stone requested writing materials and sent a letter to General McClellan requesting information about the charges related to his arrest. Of course, McClellan had known that Stone might be arrested for several weeks. He had done his best to delay the action, but when it was clear that powerful political forces were at work against Stone, McClellan did nothing to stand in the way of the inevitable. Eventually, General Stone was given back the contents of his pockets and placed in the custody of two government agents who would accompany him as he made his way north toward New York on the Baltimore and Ohio Railroad. In perhaps the saddest footnote to his arrest, when Stone's train reached Philadelphia and required the purchase of a new transfer ticket, the two agents did not have enough cash to cover the cost of Stone's fare, and he was forced to pay his own way. Stone, ever the obliging officer, thereupon paid the cost of his rail ticket to prison.[215]

Months later, in a letter addressed to army adjutant general Lorenzo Thomas on September 25, 1862, Stone bitterly recalled the humiliating details of his arrest, writing:

> *During the night of February 9 I was conveyed, in charge of a lieutenant and two police officers, to Fort Lafayette, New York Harbor, and turned over to the custody of Lieut. Col. Martin Burke, Third Artillery, who immediately sent me in charge of a guard…where I was delivered to Lieutenant Wood, Ninth Infantry. The money was taken from my pockets, and I was placed in solitary confinement in a room ordinarily used as enlisted-men's quarters, where I was kept forty-nine days, no letter being allowed to reach or leave me without inspection.…After forty-nine days I was transferred to Fort Hamilton, and allowed opportunities of obtaining air and exercise, but the same restrictions were continued on my correspondence.*

Stone remained in confinement for 189 days.[216]

Many of the officers who had served under Stone's command were appalled by his arrest and the puffed-up claims of disloyalty. Brigadier General Gorman wrote that Stone had his "entire confidence as a true, loyal patriot," and that he would be happy to "attack or defend [under his] military skill and judgement." Lieutenant Henry L. Abbott wrote that "to doubt his loyalty is simply ridiculous. I wouldn't send a private to the guard house on such absurd charges."[217] Captain Clinton Berry of the Eighty-Second New York Infantry testified before the committee that the soldiers had great confidence in General Stone. He related that "the better informed portion of the army, that is, the educated men, have great confidence in General Stone" and added,

> *In regard to my own opinion of General Stone, I think he is certainly one of the most accomplished soldiers and gentlemen that I have ever had the pleasure to meet. His management of his division shows that. He is constantly bringing into effect changes to make our volunteers equal to the regulars. He follows the army regulations a little to* [sic] *strict for volunteers, perhaps, but I think it is out of regard to our own interests.*[218]

Colonel Cogswell of the Tammany Regiment and Lieutenant Colonel Wistar also defended Stone. Wistar wrote: "If General Stone is a traitor, there are no true men." The Union army's former commanding general Winfield Scott echoed Wistar's statement of confidence in Stone: "If he is a traitor I am a traitor, and we are all traitors."[219]

The news of Stone's arrest also spread quickly through the ranks, and not all of the men were supportive of General Stone. In a letter from Poolesville, Maryland, on February 15, 1862, to "Friends at Home," Private Solomon B. Clark of the Thirty-Fourth New York Volunteer Infantry wrote, "You have undoubtedly heard of Gen. Stone's arrest and that he is now confined in Fort Lafayette." Although Private Clark's regiment was not directly engaged in the Battle of Ball's Bluff, he added: "That very thing has made the troops under his command feel as glad as though they had won a battle. It is certainly the best thing that could have been done in my estimation."[220]

Although Stone repeatedly tried to discern the charges that had precipitated his arrest, such information was not forthcoming. On the day after his arrest, Stone sent a note to General Seth Williams, McClellan's adjutant general, requesting a copy of the charges against him. When General Williams did not respond to his inquiry, Stone wrote directly to the War Department. This letter also went unanswered, and Stone soon realized that there were powerful forces at work against him. Although Stone had not been known to court politically influential friends during his military career, he now understood that his situation required special measures.[221] Stone tried to enlist the assistance of his most powerful friends in securing his release but was hampered by the War Department restrictions on his correspondence. A number of Stone's allies in the U.S. Senate succeeded in securing approval of a legislative resolution demanding an explanation of Stone's arrest by the secretary of war but this also went unanswered.

Stone's brother-in-law and lawyer Henry Melville Parker tried for weeks to gain a personal interview with Secretary Stanton, only to suffer a frustrating series of canceled appointments. On February 19 and 20, Parker finally met with Stanton, who was unmoved by Parker's arguments and suggested that he had far more important things to worry about than the fate of an imprisoned general.[222]

While army regulations provided that soldiers could be held under arrest for only eight days without benefit of court-martial, no official charges were ever leveled against General Stone. When asked to intercede on Stone's behalf, President Lincoln indicated in a letter dated May 1, 1862, that Stone had not been tried because, "in the state of military operations at the time of his arrest and since, the officers to constitute a court-martial and for witnesses could not be withdrawn from duty without injury to the service." The president's reluctance to become involved in Stone's case is curious. While some historians have suggested that the illness of Lincoln's children during the period (his son Willie died on February 20) may have caused the president to distance himself from such matters, others have reasoned that Lincoln may have harbored resentment toward Stone because of Baker's death. Regardless of his motivation, Lincoln did not intervene on Stone's behalf and became involved only after a second resolution approved by the U.S. Senate on April 21, 1862, specifically requested that he inform the Senate of the details of Stone's arrest. Lincoln replied generally and cautiously to the Senate request, promising that Stone would "be allowed a trial without any unnecessary delay" and that "the charges and specifications will be furnished him in due season."[223]

No charges were ever filed. Despite President Lincoln's assertion that charges and specifications would be furnished "in due season," General Stone was never formally charged, never provided with the details of the evidence presented against him and never tried.

This frustrating reality, however, did not stop those anxious to find General Stone responsible for Ball's Bluff from shamelessly crafting their own fanciful charges against the beleaguered general. On February 13, 1862, the *Evansville Daily Journal* reported that General Stone had been arrested and sent to Fort Lafayette based "on the following charges:

> *1st For misbehavior at Ball's Bluff*
> *2d Holding correspondence with the enemy before and since the battle of Ball's Bluff and receiving visits from rebel officers in his camp.*
> *3d For treacherously suffering the enemy to build a fort near the battle of*

> *Ball's Bluff under his gaze unmolested.*
> *4th Of a design to expose his force to capture by the enemy under pretense of orders for moving from the Commanding General.*

Ultimately, it took an act of Congress to secure Stone's release. California's junior senator James McDougall, an old friend of Stone's, had been working hard to secure Stone's release, only to be frustrated at every turn. It was Senator McDougall who identified a loophole in a military appropriations bill that finally brought relief to Stone, offered as an amendment to a noncontroversial military pay bill; McDougall submitted language stipulating that it was unlawful to hold an officer under arrest for more than thirty days without trial. The measure was approved on July 17, 1862. Although this amendment was clearly offered to address Stone's situation and to secure his immediate release, Secretary of War Stanton applied the measure literally and maliciously and refused to free Stone until thirty days following the effective date of the legislation. As a result, Stone did not gain his release until August 16, 1862.[224]

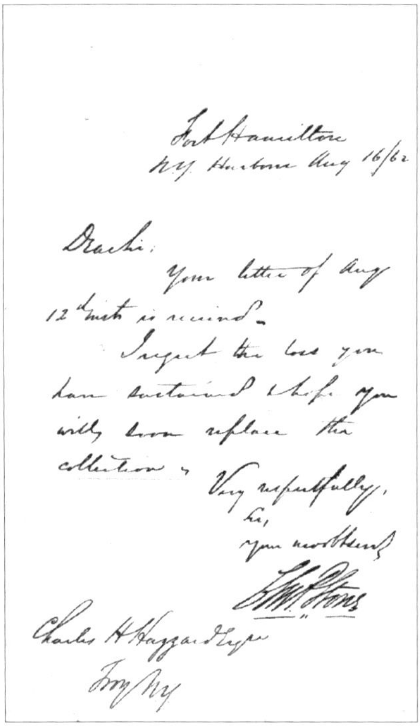
Fort Hamilton
N.Y. Harbor Aug 16/62

Dear Sir:
Your letter of Aug 12th inst is received.
I regret the loss you have sustained & hope you will soon replace the collection.
Very respectfully,
Sir,
your most obedt
C.P. Stone

Charles H Haggard Esqr
Troy NY

Letter from General Stone Sent on the day of his release from prison. *Author's collection.*

In reviewing the actions of Secretary of War Stanton, at least one biographer has suggested that the treatment of General Stone was atypical of the great power that Secretary Stanton wielded after joining the Lincoln administration. Stanton's initial response to the amendment by Senator McDougall was to ignore it and the amendment's further demand of accountability from the Secretary of War. Massachusetts senator Henry Wilson had largely muted the action against Stanton by requiring President Lincoln to detail the issues surrounding Stone's arrest, but Lincoln largely restated for Congress what Secretary Stanton had already told him. Even when Stone was eventually released, Stanton justified his delayed action based on the excuse that he had been waiting for the scheduling of a court-martial proceeding that could not be convened within the required timeframe.[225]

Even after Stone's release from incarceration, the secretary of war continued to frustrate the general. Since Stone's real offense may have been the insults to Senator Sumner, Stanton took repeated actions against Stone to appease Sumner and the Radical Republican hierarchy. Stanton blocked every attempt by General Stone to seek new assignment, effectively delaying his return by six months. The actions of the secretary of war, permitted by President Lincoln, were manifested by the extraordinary powers the president vested in his war secretary. The nineteenth-century historian and Lincoln supporter Alexander McClure observed that Stanton's abuses of power compromised Lincoln's legacy, observing: "It will be regretted by the impartial historian of the future that Stanton was capable of impressing his intense hatred so conspicuously upon the annals of the country, and that Lincoln, in several memorable instances, failed to reverse his War Minister when he had grave doubts about the wisdom or justice of his methods."[226]

While an officer in the modern army subjected to such indignity would likely resign his commission and retain an attorney to file suit, Stone lived in an era when honor and duty held transcendental meaning. In typical fashion, following his release from imprisonment, Stone reported for duty. When no assignment was offered, Stone wrote to General McClellan requesting assignment. McClellan's solicitation of War Department guidance failed to elicit a response, and the Union army commander was soon concerned with other matters as he sought to counter Confederate general Robert E. Lee's invasion into Maryland. Lee's offensive and the resulting battle at Antietam in September 1862 proved McClellan's downfall. Frustrated by his wavering and ever-complaining general, President Lincoln removed him from command of the Army of the Potomac in early November. General Stone was undeterred by the dissonant swirl of national events and the apparent lack of interest in his situation. Convinced that he still had much to offer the Union cause, he initiated a relentless correspondence with government officials he believed were involved in his case, but, in almost every instance, he was frustrated by their lack of cooperation with his mission to clear his name and gain a new active-duty assignment.

Stone did eventually get an audience with President Lincoln. When Stone asked the president what factors inspired his arrest and incarceration, President Lincoln indicated that the arrest had been made upon his "general authority." He then told Stone that he had never questioned his loyalty and referred him to General Henry Halleck for further guidance in securing a duty assignment. Halleck, the consummate government bureaucrat, obfuscated and offered no meaningful assistance. He reminded Stone that he was no longer under arrest and that no charges were pending but offered no other clarification or further orders. Stone was tired of the double-talk.

Major General Nathaniel P. Banks. *Author's collection.*

Back in January 1862, Stone had been provided with a final opportunity to review the testimony against him and make a direct response. He provided detailed testimony that refuted much of what had been said against him. Stone left the hearing room convinced that he had effectively articulated his case and, at long last, restored his reputation. The committee, however, was unmoved. Instead of making any conclusion about the case in favor of Stone, they simply compiled all of the testimony to let the public, and history, be the judge. On April 6, 1863, the Committee on the Conduct of the War published its full report on the Ball's Bluff investigation. The *National Republican* newspaper in Washington, D.C., wrote that the report offered "little new light" thrown "upon the causes of the disaster."[227] It provided no explanation for why formal charges were not offered against General Stone, concluding: "The evidence is so contradictory that your committee refrains from expressing any positive opinion upon that point, but allow each one to form his own conclusion from the testimony they have been able to obtain." It was a backhanded and insufficient exoneration of General Stone.[228]

The *New York Times* criticized the work of the committee, writing: "The whole chapter, from beginning to end, has been as impenetrable as the veil of Isis. There was something behind, but that was all that could be made out.…As it is, Gen. Stone has sustained a most flagrant wrong—a wrong which will probably stand as the worst blot on the National side in the history of the war."[229]

Stone did not return to the army until May 1863, when he was sent to the Department of the Gulf to serve as the chief of staff to General Nathaniel P. Banks. Banks, a former governor of Massachusetts, was a general well versed in politics. He had come to Stone's support following the collapse of the Union line at Ball's Bluff and now tried to help Stone once again, this time with an opportunity for redemption. Although Stone performed commendable staff officer's service during Banks's unsuccessful Red River Campaign of 1863, Stone was recalled to Washington before the campaign was complete. As Stone was assigned to the headquarters of the Army of the Potomac, the army's new commander, Lieutenant General U.S. Grant tried to find a suitable position for him. Before this could take place, however, Stone was stripped of his brigadier general's commission and reduced in to the rank of colonel. The official action was initiated by the War Department, but it was actually Stone's old nemesis, Senator Charles Sumner, who privately took credit for the reduction in rank. In August, General Grant gave Stone a brigade in the Army of the Potomac's Fifth Corps, but his tenure was short-lived. On September 8, 1864, Stone tendered his resignation. While waiting for his resignation to be accepted, Stone seems to have undergone something of a mental breakdown and sent a strange message to Major General G. Gordon Meade, requesting to be "shot by your order tomorrow." Stone wrote that any officer accused of what he had been accused of "had no right to live and I earnestly request that my execution may be ordered." Stone's resignation from the army he had served so loyally was made effective on September 13, 1864.[230]

The personal impact of Ball's Bluff on General Stone went far beyond his health-compromising imprisonment, the public criticism of his military leadership or even his eventual mental breakdown. In October 1862, his mother-in-law died, and in February 1863, just a month after his third and final appearance before the Committee on the Conduct of the War, his wife passed away, leaving him with a daughter to raise on his own. His wife was just thirty-one years old, and her loss devastated Stone. Perhaps the toll was just too much for them. Stone struggled to find a position that would help him regain the high stature he once enjoyed. He married a young woman he met while serving in Louisiana and fathered two children with her, but full redemption proved elusive.[231]

After his resignation, General Stone returned to Massachusetts to recuperate and restore his health. He traveled to Mexico and accepted a position after the war with a coal-mining firm based in Richmond, Virginia. In 1869, and based on the recommendation of his old friend, General William T. Sherman, Stone accepted a position as chief of staff to the Egyptian army. In this position, Stone explored the Nile and improved the Egyptian military forces. He also worked with many Confederate veterans who exported their military skills to other countries. For a short time, Colonel Walter Jenifer, who had commanded the Confederate cavalry at Ball's Bluff, served as Egypt's inspector of cavalry.[232] Stone remained in service until 1883, when the British assumed control of the country. Stone returned to the United States, served as an engineer in Florida and became the chief engineer for the construction of the Statue of Liberty in New York Harbor. During his work on the project, he labored within site of the prison where he had once been incarcerated for his role at Ball's Bluff. Stone served as the grand marshal of the statue's dedication ceremonies in October 1886 and remained in New York City. He contracted pneumonia later that winter and died on January 24, 1887. He was buried with full military honors at West Point.[233]

9

"The Absurdity of the Thing"

Original sketch of bodies from Ball's Bluff Drawn by *Harper's* war artist A.R. Waud. *Library of Congress.*

The small party of men under the guidance of Dr. John Barclay Crawford had come to the Ball's Bluff battlefield on a mission. Dr. Crawford, who served as an assistant surgeon to the Fifty-Second Pennsylvania Reserves, was charged by the State of Pennsylvania to investigate the battlefield of Ball's Bluff and locate the graves of Pennsylvania soldiers lost in the fight. The hope was that the remains of the soldiers could be brought back to Pennsylvania for reburial. Upon his arrival, Dr. Crawford was shocked by what he found there in April 1862.

In walking the former field of battle, Dr. Crawford found the bodies of fallen Union soldiers in an "advanced stage of decomposition" that "utterly precluded any attempt at their removal." Crawford reported that he "found the bodies of our killed…deposited in various places; some in isolated graves…but [that] most had been promiscuously placed in washes formed by recent water currents on the battle-ground. They had been but superficially covered with earth, and some of the bodies were exposed. Some had been

Dr. John Barclay Crawford visited the Battlefield in April 1862. *Collection of Ken Fleming.*

mutilated." Unable to determine the identities, or even the regiments that the fallen men belonged to, Dr. Crawford decided to leave the bodies where they were found. In his report to the Pennsylvania surgeon general, Dr. Crawford noted that he reburied "the detached portions of bodies in the places from which they had been removed, and covered them properly with earth and stones [to protect against] their future exposure."[234]

It had been a sad duty, and Crawford promised that "satisfactory assurances" had been made by the people of Leesburg that the burials would be respected. The cost of Dr. Crawford's expedition was less than seventy-five dollars.[235]

What was referred to dismissively as "the Leesburg affair" started out as a routine reconnaissance aimed at discovering Confederate intentions along the Upper Potomac. While there was much to be gained in learning such information as the armies settled into quarters for the first winter of the war, it was thought that the movement might compel the abandonment of the town of Leesburg by the small Confederate force garrisoned there. Through a bizarre set of circumstances understood by few of those who had roles in the drama, the operation achieved an importance far beyond the simple scouting mission envisioned by the Union army commanders.

The Union force had taken up a position ill-suited for battle or effective defense and was led by a politician–turned–military officer who gained his rank not through formal tactical education or experience on the battlefield but as a result of his political connections. A fierce battle had been fought and then lost and young lives sacrificed in ways that the adventure-seeking volunteers who enlisted in the spring of 1861 could scarcely have imagined. Quite bluntly, more Union soldiers died from incompetence than bullets at Ball's Bluff. So many of those who perished drowned in the swift currents of the Potomac. The nation might embrace the imagery of heroic death on the battlefield and perhaps even accept disease and sickness in camp, but the

Union soldiers who were lost at Ball's Bluff died because the inexperienced officers in command had bungled the operation. The newspaper reports of the battle made it clear that most of the soldiers had died because not enough boats had been secured for effective transport.

The World, a New York weekly newspaper, published an account of the fight on November 2, 1861. The report, filed by a special correspondent on October 28, was heavily influenced by conversations with Captain Francis Young, but observed:

> *The transit of a broad, unbridged river, by a modern army, has been deemed a serious undertaking. Pontoon bridges, built by engineers—with all scientific strength and appliance—or scores of great bateaux are required to make good the absence of steam ferriage for the conveyance of artillery, army wagons, horses, the army itself, and its cumbersome necessities and implements.*[236]

The correspondent concluded: "The attempt to cross a rapid river in any force, with such small means of ferriage and at such a point as this, except from some desperate, impelling exigency, is without precedent, and utterly incomprehensible."[237]

On the day following the battle, Lieutenant Henry Abbott of the Twentieth Massachusetts Infantry reflected on the tragedy in a letter to his parents:

> *Now look at the absurdity of the thing. To cross the river we had two row boats that together carried over 30 men at a time. We landed on the hill* [which was] *about perpendicular & thickly wooded. When we got on the top, we are drawn up on the only open space there is, about wide enough for a front of two regiments, & about a short rifle shot in length, surrounded on every side by large, unexplored woods. It was in fact one of the most complete slaughter pens ever devised.*[238]

Ball's Bluff was surely an absurdity, and the painful retelling of battle's human costs did little to assuage public outrage. But the accusatory assertions of the politicians demanding accountability for the disaster rang hollow. The foundation for their inquiry was eagerness to defend the memory of one of their own rather than to discover truth. With General McClellan still holding the confidence of President Lincoln and Colonel Baker dead, there was no one left to blame for the Ball's Bluff debacle but General Stone. The beleaguered officer became a target of political and public ire. The congressional investigation did nothing to ensure that another Ball's Bluff–type failure would not occur upon some other field in the coming months. Instead, while Senators and Congressmen postured and skittish military leaders cowered, the Union cause floundered in a manner that tested the nation's very social, political and military core. There were lessons of command and tactics that could have been learned from a more objective review. Such an investigation, rather than an inquisition, might have redeemed the costly legacy of Ball's Bluff, but that opportunity was lost, ignored by the easy and concerted political effort to ruin General Stone and bring quick closure to the sad story.

Union major general G. Gordon Meade, who later commanded the Army of the Potomac at Gettysburg and through the grinding Virginia campaigns of 1864, had a minor role at Ball's Bluff. He had led a brigade in General McCall's division that had made the advance on Dranesville. Considering the Ball's Bluff fiasco just a few days after the battle, Meade had written privately in a letter to his wife:

> *Regarding Ball's Bluff, as far as I can gather, the whole affair was a bungle from beginning to end. The worst part of the business is that at the very time our people were contending against such odds, the advance of McCall's division was only 10 miles off and had we been ordered forward instead of back, we could have captured the whole of them.*[239]

Criticism of the operation abounded. While many newspapers, whether targeting President Lincoln or General McClellan, used Ball's Bluff to question the administration of the war, a few tried to shore up the trembling confidence of the Northern population. The popular illustrated newspaper *Harper's Weekly* was the most widely read periodical of the war, achieving a circulation of about 200,000. The paper's November 9, 1861 issue published an editorial that tried to bolster the Union war effort in the face of the defeats at Big Bethel, First Manassas and Ball's Bluff. It reads:

> *Citizens of the United States, what our country needs now of you is pluck, a little pluck. It is not expected that you should emulate the citizens of Rome, who passed a vote of thanks to Varro, fresh from the overwhelming defeat of Cannae, "for that he had not despaired of the republic," but it is hoped that you will not allow two-penny reverses to disappoint you, or turn your animosity to expect that, in the course of the war, all our generals will meet with reverses. What is wanted of the people is that they should not lose heart on this account, that they should not denounce a general because he has been*

> *beaten; that they should not heed the ignorant criticisms—after the fact—of babbling editors who have never seen a battle-field; but that with a large faith in the righteousness of our cause, and the ultimate triumph of law, order, good government and democracy over anarchy, rebellion and negro slavery, they should cheerfully submit to the stripes which fate may lay upon them, and should feel confident of the truth of their principles under defeat as in success. If the people will vouchsafe this, the army will do the rest.*[240]

It was not just newspapers loyal to the Union cause that urged confidence in the wake of defeat. From camp at Winchester, Virginia, on March 17, 1862, Private Theodore G. Goff of the Fifth Connecticut Infantry wrote to his mother and tried to lift her spirits about the progress of the war:

> *You have got the wrong idea about the War thinking that it looks worse every day. It looks very bright to me and I will tell you why. Every place we take it makes the enemy so much the weaker. I tell you what it is, Sesh* [secessionists] *are about played out. They'll run like sheep before us. You say you think they are trapping us but General McClellan is too smart for them. He is not going to rush on them without any fore thought and have another Bull Run and Balls Bluff affair, but he is going to have his Army of the Potomac move very slowly along and secure every place we take. The citizens seem to receive us with joy.*[241]

For his part, General McClellan did all that he could to distance himself from the controversy surrounding the battle. In his report of his operations in Virginia and Maryland in the first year of the war, McClellan only briefly discussed the Ball's Bluff fight in an account that was sprinkled with sections culled from joint committee testimony that served his interest. McClellan wrote that he did not order General Stone to cross the Potomac but only to "make some display of an intention to cross, and also to watch the enemy more closely than usual."[242] In order to leave no doubt regarding culpability, McClellan added: "I did not direct [Stone] to cross, nor did I intend that he should cross the river in force for the purpose of fighting."[243] Concluding his account with edited sections from Stone's testimony before the joint committee that absolved McClellan of responsibility, McClellan closed his brief recounting of the battle with the suggestion that further information could be obtained from General Stone's report of the battle that had been furnished to the War Department and Stone's testimony to the Committee on the Conduct of the War.[244]

More than a century and a half after the guns fell silent at Ball's Bluff, historians often remain focused on the issue of leadership responsibility and argue the tactical aspects of the battle not just to document the ebb and flow of troop movements, but to answer the nagging question of "Who is to blame?" It is as if, in the end, the politicians who formed the Committee on the Conduct of the War prevailed in enforcing their conclusion as to what is and is not important in understanding the battle's meaning and legacy. It is as if nothing has been learned from the tragedy at Ball's Bluff, forcing the dead that drift up in memory to remain forever restless in their graves.

Although historians are generally quick to reject the findings of the Committee on the Conduct of War, preferring to assign responsibility to other officers involved who were not targeted by the politically tinged work of the committee, the burden of responsibility for what happened at Ball's Bluff cannot be wholly borne by any individual commander. It was a combination of factors that led to the Union defeat. The collective failings and weaknesses of Union officers, the geography of the battlefield, the odd turns of fate and the tactical success of the Confederate leadership were all factors that contributed to the historical outcome. To argue differently ignores the legacy of Ball's Bluff and encourages the same simplistic conclusions that forever taint the work of the Committee on the Conduct of the War. The undoubtedly heroic but unquestionably inexperienced Colonel Baker offers as convincing a scapegoat for Ball's Bluff as General Stone, but Baker's military incompetence can only partly account for the catastrophe that saw panicked Union troops flee from the field of battle. Similarly, General George B. McClellan, who has been criticized for his self-preserving role in the battle's storyline, cannot be saddled with the full weight of responsibility for the battle's outcome. While McClellan gave impetus to the operation by ordering General Stone to make a "slight demonstration," as overall commander of the Union army in the East, he had little direct command control of the field of battle or the small force that was engaged there. Indeed, McClellan was far removed from the battlefield and provided with only sporadic reports of fighting by his subordinate officers on the field. While McClellan certainly could have done better in coordinating McCall's advance on Dranesville with Stone's demonstration and could have kept Stone more properly informed of McCall's operation, the two movements were not contemporaneously viewed as part of a single offensive operation. The lost opportunities offered by a more coordinated campaign between the forces are only apparent in hindsight and in the wake of the battle that Baker fought at Ball's Bluff.

The Congressional Committee on the Conduct of the War investigated the role of the key players in the Ball's Bluff operation and, more for the political reasons previously discussed, placed the burden of the catastrophe squarely on the shoulders of General Stone. While Stone's political inexperience and McClellan's remarkable facility for extricating himself from any responsibility in the disaster hastened Stone's professional demise, the congressional committee also expressed the deep frustrations of the public when it punished General Stone for the Union defeat at Ball's Bluff. In reviewing the history of the battle, some historians have reacted to this politically tinged congressional inquisition by absolving General Stone of all responsibility for the failure at Ball's Bluff. While the intensity and purpose of the congressional effort to discredit Stone and the treatment he received at the hands of his accusers following his arrest and imprisonment do not exemplify the best that the American democratic tradition has to offer, a review of Stone's military leadership at Ball's Bluff does raise serious concerns.

General McClellan's original instructions to make "a slight demonstration" along the Potomac were far exceeded by the forces under Stone's command. Had Stone resolved to end the operation after the brief action at Edward's Ferry rather than force the issue with the crossing at Ball's Bluff, a different story would undoubtedly have been written. Stone would have complied with his orders and would have preserved better options for coordination with the larger forces at hand (both McCall and Banks). Ball's Bluff became a complex operation because of the hasty manner in which it was executed and because the commanders with overall responsibility had no clear sense of what was going on once the Union forces had crossed the Potomac.

While Colonel Baker was in direct command of the operation on the field of battle, Stone allowed the fog of war to completely envelop him and can be appropriately criticized for not doing more to solicit better information about the events that were unfolding on the Virginia side of the Potomac. In addition, the use of three separate Potomac crossing sites, which resulted in the attacking Union forces remaining far out of supporting distance from each another during the fight, was a tactical blunder that Stone's inexperienced officers and troops could ill afford. Compounding the problem was Stone's fragmented and haphazard deployment of troops. The small force that Colonel Baker commanded on the field at Ball's Bluff consisted of the elements of three separate brigades that had never before fought, or even drilled, together as a single unit. With 10,000 troops at his disposal, only about 1,700 participated in the Ball's Bluff battle. While it might be argued in Stone's defense that he did not have direct control over the deployment of troops and had delegated authority of such matters to Colonel Baker, the relinquishment of such control in the presence of the enemy and the lack of command coordination and communication highlight Stone's most significant operational failings at Ball's Bluff.

In granting Colonel Baker broad discretionary authority, Stone effectively relieved himself of direct military command. As a result, Stone was unable to appreciate the seriousness of the drama that was evolving at Ball's Bluff until the first accounts of panic and flight were relayed to his headquarters. By the time he received these reports, it was too late, and his defeated force was in full retreat, struggling by any means to reach the safety of Harrison's Island. While there is good cause for the censure of Baker's conduct in not providing his promised periodic situation reports to Stone to advise him of what was happening on the battlefield, Stone must be criticized for not attempting to learn more about the progress of the operation even after he began to entertain concerns about Colonel Baker's conduct of the battle. A historian studying the factors that contributed to the outcome of a battle can build a case for Stone's noninvolvement in the tactical aspects of the Ball's Bluff operation, but common sense would dictate that, based upon the information (or lack thereof) available to him, Stone should have moved closer to the battlefront (or assigned a trusted staff officer such duty) and actively participated in the important strategic decisions of the battle.

Even under the best of circumstances, General Stone's orders for the scouting operation carried great risk. Stone, who was in the best position to ensure that the larger strategic goals of the reconnaissance were being met, was invisible on the battlefield. Stone's reluctance to involve himself more fully in the military decision-making process at Ball's Bluff exacted a high price that was measured both in the loss of life and later, public frustration with the larger issues related to the general conduct of the war. In the months following Southern secession and First Manassas, there was a general feeling on both sides that this would be a short, if not bloodless war. First Manassas proved that the war would not be so bloodless and rattled public sentiments. In the North, the combination of defeats at First Manassas and Ball's Bluff underlined the serious business of war and made it very clear that amateurish mistakes on the battlefield carried real consequences. When military commanders made mistakes, young lives were lost. The public reaction to defeat was not just measured in the dead and wounded, it also tested public confidence, both in relation to support for military leadership, as well as the larger Union cause. How long the Northern population could support a failed war effort was a question that challenged political and military

Lieutenant John "Willie" Grout of the Fifteenth Massachusetts. *Author's collection.*

authorities in the North throughout the grim winter of 1861–62.

The Union failure at Ball's Bluff produced many casualties, from the influential and ambitious Colonel Edward D. Baker to the beleaguered General Charles Stone and even the young eighteen-year-old Lieutenant "Willie" Grout of the Fifteenth Massachusetts Infantry. Grout, whose death in the battle was remembered by the nation in the haunting verses of one of the war's most moving and popular songs, "The Vacant Chair," became a symbol for all who were lost in those first months of war.

In the long string of defeats that marked the rocky path of the Army of the Potomac, Ball's Bluff was soon forgotten. There would be other blunders on other fields that would result in the loss of even larger numbers of Union soldiers, and Ball's Bluff slowly receded in memory. Heading into the first winter of the war in 1861, the military, and indeed the nation at large, could scarcely conceive of the horrors that awaited them at places such as Shiloh, Antietam, Fredericksburg, Chancellorsville and Gettysburg. The names of these places would soon become seared into the national consciousness.

These great battles of the war would all come later. In the wake of Ball's Bluff, the Union and Confederate armies prepared for the winter ahead and the prospect of renewed campaigns in the spring. Ball's Bluff had done little to change the strategic disposition of the two armies, and a pessimistic soldier of the ranks might have wondered whether the battle had served any purpose at all, for all its terrible pain and suffering. Back in Boston, Oliver Wendell Holmes Jr. recuperated from the chest wound he received and spent the season reflecting on his comrades who had perished on the field of battle. He found himself celebrated as a hero, and from his room in his parent's elegant Beacon Hill residence, Holmes was compelled to retell the story of the fight as visitors came to his bedside. Holmes soon grew restless, however, and the same spirit that motivated him to rise to his feet after he received his first wound at Ball's Bluff inspired him to return to his regiment. Despite the seriousness of his wound and his incomplete recovery, Holmes was back in the ranks by late January 1863 and prepared to "see the thing through."[245]

The Eighth Virginia Infantry also spent much of the winter thinking about Ball's Bluff. Their brave flag bearer, Sergeant Clinton Hatcher, had fallen in the fight. It was to his memory that the regiment accepted a new regimental battle flag made by General Beauregard's wife from one of her own silk dresses. In presenting the flag to the unit, General Beauregard noted that it was in recognition "for distinguished valor on the field of battle at Ball's Bluff."[246]

Although the memory of the battle was soon eclipsed by the more vivid remembrances of the action on other battlefields, what took place at Ball's Bluff continued to haunt the spirits of many. Toward the close of the war, the struggling novelist Herman Melville published a book of poems titled *Battle-Pieces,* chronicling the history of the war in verse. When Melville tried to evoke the feeling of the shattering moment of the transformation of Northern patriotic optimism to a fuller recognition of the Civil War's terrible realities, he returned to the sad legacy of Ball's Bluff:

One noonday, at my window in the town,
I saw a sight—saddest that eyes can see—
Young soldiers marching lustily
Unto the wars,
With fifes, flags in mottoed pageantry;
While all the porches, walks and doors
Were rich with ladies cheering royally.

They moved like Juny morning on the wave,
Their hearts were fresh as clover in its prime
(it was the breezy summer time),
Life throbbed some strong,
How should they dream that Death in a rosy clime
Would come to thin their shining throng?
Youth feels immortal, like the gods sublime.
Weeks passed; and at my window, leaving bed,
By night I mused, of easeful sleep bereft,
On those brave boys (Ah War! thy theft);
Some marching feet
Found pause at last by cliffs Potomac cleft;
Wakeful I mused, while in the street
Far footfalls died away till none were left[247]

Order of Battle, October 1861

Stone's Division, Army of the Potomac (Brigadier General Charles P. Stone)

1st Brigade (Brigadier General Willis A. Gorman)

2nd New York State Militia (later redesignated 82nd New York Infantry)
1st Minnesota Infantry
15th Massachusetts Infantry
34th New York Infantry
42nd New York Infantry (known as the Tammany Regiment)

2nd Brigade (Brigadier General Frederick W. Lander)

19th Massachusetts Infantry
20th Massachusetts Infantry
7th Michigan Infantry
1st Company, Massachusetts Sharpshooters

3rd Brigade (Colonel Edward D. Baker)

1st California Infantry (later redesignated 71st Pennsylvania)
2nd California Infantry (later redesignated 69th Pennsylvania)
3rd California Infantry (later redesignated 72d Pennsylvania)
4th California Infantry (later redesignated 106th Pennsylvania)

Cavalry

3rd New York Cavalry (six companies)
Putnam Rangers (later redesignated Company L, 1st Maryland Cavalry)

Artillery

Battery I, 1st United States Artillery
Battery B, 1st Rhode Island Light Artillery
Battery K, 9th New York State Militia (later 6th Independent Battery, NY Light Artillery)

CONFEDERATE FORCES

7th Brigade, First Corps, Army of the Potomac, CSA (Colonel Nathan G. Evans)

13th Mississippi Infantry
17th Mississippi Infantry
18th Mississippi Infantry
8th Virginia Infantry

Cavalry (Lieutenant Colonel Walter H. Jenifer

Companies B, C and E, 4th Virginia Cavalry
Company K, 6th Virginia Cavalry

Artillery

1st Company, Richmond Howitzers

Appendix A

Union and Confederate Casualties at Ball's Bluff

The casualty tables reproduced in this section are based upon a number of sources, including the U.S. War Department's *Official Records of the Union and Confederate Armies*, published in 1909. This early compendium provided an official count of the Union killed in action of just 49. *The Medical and Surgical History of the War of the Rebellion*, published in 1870, provided a figure of 223 Union soldiers killed in action. The Civil War Trust, an organization dedicated to battlefield preservation, cited Union loss figures for Ball's Bluff of 223 killed, 226 wounded and 553 missing and captured, for a total of 1,002 casualties. While every effort has been made to revise the loss tables for the Union and Confederates forces engaged at Ball's Bluff, based on muster roll and other regimental data, the incomplete nature of military record keeping at the time of the Civil War frustrates efforts to compile a definitive statistical record.

In formulating this revised list, the author examined both regimental and individual soldier records in the holdings of the National Archives, the New York State Archives and the New York State Military Museum and Veterans Research Center. It should be noted that in considering the loss tables for the Union force at Ball's Bluff, the casualties constitute a combined loss from all causes of more than 51 percent of the estimated 1,720 Union soldiers who fought in the battle. An analysis of these original records serves as the basis for the following revised loss tables:

UNION CASUALTIES AT BALL'S BLUFF

	KILLED		WOUNDED		MISSING		TOTAL
	O	E	O	E	O	E	
15th Massachusetts	2	33	3	62	7	125	232
20th Massachusetts	3	36	6	42	5	108	200
42nd New York	3	24	2	11	5	118	163
California Regiment	3	23	3	37	7	236	309
6th New York Battery	—	—	1	—	—	—	1
1st R.I. Battery	—	—	—	5	—	4	9
1st U.S. Artillery	—	—	1	—	—	—	1
TOTAL	**11**	**116**	**16**	**157**	**24**	**591**	**915**

O = Officers
E = Enlisted

CONFEDERATE CASUALTIES AT BALL'S BLUFF

	KILLED		WOUNDED		MISSING		TOTAL
	O	E	O	E	O	E	
13th Mississippi	1	3	—	2	—	1	7
17th Mississippi	2	—	1	8	—	—	11
18th Mississippi	—	22	7	56	—	—	85
8th Virginia	—	8	4	39	1	—	52
TOTAL	**3**	**33**	**12**	**105**	**1**	**1**	**155**

O = Officers
E = Enlisted

Appendix B

Roster of the Union Soldiers Killed at Ball's Bluff

Because Confederate forces were in command of the field at the close of battle, many of the Union soldiers who fell at Ball's Bluff were buried in shallow graves by an enemy that had little opportunity or incentive to properly identify the dead. Civil War soldiers were not issued the dog tags required by the military in later conflicts, so determining the identity of the battlefield dead was extremely difficult. In fact, of the fifty-four Union soldiers buried in the government military cemetery at Ball's Bluff, only one, Private James Allen of the Fifteenth Massachusetts, is memorialized by an individual headstone. It is likely that the remains of many Union soldiers still rest in forgotten graves on the Ball's Bluff battlefield.

Complicating the task of accurately identifying the dead was the nature of the battle. Contemporary accounts suggest that the highest number of casualties probably occurred as a result of the flight of the Union troops from their position atop the bluff to the riverbank below. Most of the soldiers listed as killed and many of those listed as missing were likely drowned in the Potomac in the attempt to reach Harrison's Island. Their bodies were carried far downstream, where they were either recovered in the months following Ball's Bluff or consigned to a watery grave. In honor of their service and suffering, this listing includes the names of those who died of wounds received in the battle in the weeks and months following the engagement. Separate notations indicate the date of death so as to differentiate those killed in action.

Because of the numerical inconsistences, and in tribute to the men who fought and died at Ball's Bluff, this listing of the Union soldiers who perished in the fight is provided as follows:

Fifteenth Massachusetts Volunteer Infantry

Allen, James, Private, Company D
Belknap, Alonzo B., Private, Company B
Benjamin, George F., Private, Company B
Buffum, Cincinatus, Private, Company K
Cowdrey, Andrew, Corporal, Company A
Cummings, Stillman L., Private, Company D
Cutler, George W., Private, Company C
Dexter, Ferdinand, Sergeant, Company F
Dickinson, Francis H., Private, Company F
Gatchell, Moses W., Captain, Company K
Goff, Charles, Private, Company D
Grout, John William, Second Lieutenant, Company D
Hilton, James, Private, Company E
Jennison, Joseph Jr., Private, Company E
Keith, Eugene, Private, Company H
Kirchner, John, Private, Company C
Lawrence, Willard R., Private, Company C
Mann, William, Private, Company H
Messinger, David J., Private, Company H
Newton, Elmer M., Private, Company G
Philips, George G., Private, Company G
Scott, Elijah M., Private, Company B
Scott, William, Private, Company I
Seaver, George F., Private, Company H
Sherman, John D., Private, Company G
Smith, John W., Private, Company D
Smith, Sidney, Private, Company F
Stafford, John F., Private, Company D
Stringer, James, Private, Company K
Taylor, George C., Corporal, Company B
Turner, Luther G., Private, Company C
Walker, John K., Private, Company B
Walker, William, Private, Company C
Warner, James G., Private, Company C
Whalen, John, Private, Company K

Twentieth Massachusetts Volunteer Infantry

Babo, Alois, Captain, Company C
Barber, Alexander M., Private, Company I (died November 21, 1861)
Brewer, Henry, Private, Company H
Burke, Patrick, Private, Company G (died November 18, 1861)
Collyer, James H., Private, Company A (died November 27, 1861)
Davis, Benjamin, Private, Company I
Dunn, Edward P., Private, Company H
Dwyer, John, Private, Company H
Eames, Warren F., Private, Company D
Galligan, James, Private, Company D
Hathaway, William R., Private, Company H (died November 27, 1861)
Kelly, George F., Private, Company A
Leonard, William A., Private, Company E
Meader, George H., Private, Company G
Merchant, John, Sergeant, Company A
Meyer, Joseph, Private, Company C
McCullough, Patrick, Private, Company D
McDermott, Patrick, Private, Company A (died January 4, 1862)
McDonough, Patrick, Private, Company D
McGoldrick, John, Private, Company G
McKay, John P., Sergeant, Company G
McKenna, Peter, Private, Company I
Murphy, Michael, Private, Company E
O'Brien, Daniel, Private, Company D
Partridge, Amos H., Private, Company D
Porter, Calvin, Private, Company D
Putnam, William L., Second Lieutenant, Company E
Roach, Daniel J., Private, Company G
Sampson, Frank, Private, Company D (died November 3, 1861)
Shine, Dennis, Private, Company G
Simpson, George E., Corporal, Company G
Snell, Joseph, Private, Company H
Stackpole, Albert, Private, Company H
Tripp, Ebenezer, Corporal, Company G
Waters, George W., Corporal, Company A
Welch, William, Private, Company A

Wesselhoeft, Reinhold, Second Lieutenant, Company C
Wire, Joseph, Private, Company D
Worth, George E., Private, Company I
Wright, Charles, Private, Company A

First California Regiment

Booth, Harry, Private, Company A
Brown, Girard A., Private, Company C
Castor, John, Private, Company D
Coggsville, James, Corporal, Company C
Connelly, Albert, Private, Company C
Chipman, David, Private, Company D
Davis, George W., Private, Company C
Gravenstein, James L., Private, Company C
Hawvy, John R., Private, Company H
Hooper, Andrew J., Private, Company A
Jaggard, Charles, Private, Company H
Johnson, John, Private, Company H
Lane, William H., Sergeant, Company C
McKim, William R., Corporal, Company A
Mullineaux, Samuel, Private, Company C
Otter, William E., Captain, Company C
Potter, Robert H. Private, Company C
Randell, Sewell, Corporal, Company D
Reynolds, John, Private, Company G
Scott, John, Private, Company D
Smith, Robert, Private, Company D
Stradling, M.L., Private, Company H
Survey, John B., Private, Company H
Tack, Oliver B., Private, Company C
Williams, Joseph D., Second Lieutenant, Company D

Forty-Second New York (Tammany) Infantry

Alden, Henry H., Captain, Company H
Bailey, Thomas, Private, Company A
Blake, George, Private, Company K
Bopp, Frederick, Private, Company K
Cahill, John, Private, Company K
Cannon, James, Private, Company A
Collins, Patrick, Private, Company K
Connor, James, Private, Company K
Danver, James, Corporal, Company K
Dennan, James, Private, Company K
Douglas, James, Private, Company A
Draddy, Terrence, Private, Company K
Fitzgerald, James, Private, Company E
Garetty, Michael, Captain, Company K
Gifford, James, Private, Company K
Gillis, James, First Lieutenant, Company E
Graham, Daniel, Private, Company E
McCarthy, Owen, Sergeant, Company H
McClelland, George, Private, Company A
McPhail, Duncan, Corporal, Company C
Mooney, William, Private, Company H
Odwell, Andrew A., Private, Company K
Ryan, Martin, Private, Company K
Sanders, John, Private, Company K
Sullivan, Edward, Private, Company K
Sullivan, John, Private, Company K
Wilson, John, Private, Company A

Appendix C

"We Shall Miss Him"

Following the Confederate bombardment of Fort Sumter, seventeen-year-old John "Willie" Grout, like many of his youthful contemporaries, was eager to join the military. The only son of a wealthy Worcester, Massachusetts industrialist, Grout was a student at Worcester's Highland Military Institute when the war broke out. Although his parents tried to discourage his enlistment, Willie's enthusiasm prevailed, and he gained permission to join a new infantry regiment being raised in the city under Colonel Charles Devens. In June 1861, largely as a result of his military cadet education, Grout was commissioned second lieutenant of Company D, Fifteenth Massachusetts Volunteer Infantry.

Grout impressed Colonel Devens as a competent and capable officer, and during the Battle of Ball's Bluff, Lieutenant Grout was detailed by Colonel Devens to supervise the transport of wounded from the battlefield to the field hospitals established on Harrison's Island.

Grout performed his duties with admirable skill, loading the tiny flatboat under his command with as many wounded as possible in several trips across the Potomac, all while under heavy fire. As the battle reached its climax and the panicked Union troops atop Ball's Bluff were pushed steadily toward the river, Grout gave up his place in the flatboat to a wounded man and determined to swim the 150-yard-wide channel to Harrison's Island.

According to surviving comrades, Lieutenant Grout was about halfway across the river when a Confederate rifle ball struck him in the back of his head. He struggled to swim the remaining distance, but his strength failed him, and he was taken by the current and swept away. On November 5, 1861, his body was recovered several miles downstream and was sent back to his grieving family in Worcester. The city honored its fallen son with a grand funeral procession that was attended by hundreds of Worcester's residents.

The loss of Willie Grout touched the city deeply and helped symbolize the loss that many felt in the early months of the Union war effort. One of those who knew him, Henry S. Washburn, wrote a Thanksgiving memorial verse that was published in the city newspaper and was later set to music by George F. Root, the war's most celebrated songwriter. The resulting song, a sentimental ballad titled "The Vacant Chair," became immensely popular with the soldiers and families of both North and South.

The Vacant Chair

We shall meet but we shall miss him
There will be one vacant chair
We shall linger to caress him
While we breathe our evening prayer
When a year ago we gathered
Joy was in his mild blue eye
But a golden chord was severed
And our hopes in ruin lie.

Chorus

We shall meet but we shall miss him
There will be one vacant chair
We shall linger to caress him
When we breathe our evening prayer.

At our fireside, sad and lonely
Often will the bosom swell
At remembrance of the story
How our noble Willie fell
How he strove to bear our banner
Through the thickest of the fight
And uphold our country's honor

In the strength of manhood's night.
True, they tell us wreaths of glory
Ever more will deck his brow
But this soothes the anguish only
Sweeping o'er our heartstrings now
Sleep today, o early fallen
In thy green and narrow bed
Dirges from the pine and cypress
Mingle with the tears we shed.

Appendix D

Letter from the Homefront

The uncertainty of the battlefield extracted a terrible toll on the lives of loved ones far away from the front. In the letter that follows, Mary Anna "Lizzie" Greene, a young lady in Westboro, Massachusetts, informs her parents of the reports of her husband's loss at Ball's Bluff. Research has identified the subject of this letter to be First Lieutenant Jeremiah Evarts Greene (1834–1902), who served with the Fifteenth Massachusetts Volunteer Infantry. Greene graduated from Yale College in 1853. When he joined the regiment in August 1861, he gave his occupation as lawyer. He was twenty-six years old. The *Worcester Daily Spy* reported Lieutenant Greene missing in action at the Battle of Ball's Bluff, although later reports indicated that he had been taken prisoner and was incarcerated in Richmond. Lieutenant Greene wrote a letter from Richmond dated December 4, 1861, that was published in the *Worcester Daily Spy*. In the letter, Lieutenant Greene described the harsh conditions at the prison and requested the people of Worcester, Massachusetts, to send blankets and clothing to the men:

> *The twenty four men of my company need such things more than I do and I hope something has been done already towards supplying them. They, of course, have not much money, and are confined in a large ware room without fire, unless that has been supplied them within a few days. They are furnished with course* [sic] *cotton enough to make a narrow bed for each man, and straw to fill them with, and with a thin cotton comforter each. The weather for a few days has been quite severe, so that the snow,*

of which there was a slight fall a few days ago, hardly melts in the sun at noon. A splendid supply arrived yesterday for the Fitchburg company, and you have no idea how delighted they were with it.

Lieutenant Greene was paroled in October 1862 and resigned from his regiment that same month. He returned to Worcester, where he established a long career as a newspaper editor. He remained active in veterans' affairs and attended regimental reunions until his death in 1902.

On March 29, 1883, a story published in the *Worcester Daily Spy* related an interesting tale about Lieutenant Greene and the Ball's Bluff battle. Toward the end of the battle, Lieutenant Greene was surrounded by Confederates, some of whom were threatening to kill him. A Confederate officer stepped forward and demanded Greene's surrender. Greene saluted the officer and handed over his sword to the officer identified as Captain Otho R. Singleton of the Eighteenth Mississippi Infantry. He was then taken away and ultimately incarcerated as a prisoner of war in Richmond. More than twenty years after the war, when Greene was serving as the editor of the *Daily Spy*, he visited Washington, D.C., where he met with his old adversary, now a congressman serving from Mississippi. Singleton promised to return the sword he had received on the field of battle. In a note that accompanied Greene's receipt of his sword, Congressman Singleton wrote: "The sword has suffered no damage, and is entirely fit for further service, but its owner hopes that it will never be drawn on another battlefield. It will not, however, be beaten into a plowshare, nor worked up into steel pens." With that gesture, the sword was reunited with the brave officer who carried it into battle in 1861.

In this letter, Lieutenant Greene's wife expresses the uncertainty and concern typical of many of the letters that would have passed between family members in the weeks following the battle.

Westboro, Oct. 31st 1861

Dear Mother & Father

Your letters are just received and I thank you very much for your kind sympathy for us in our deep affliction. I was sure you would remember us & that we should have your prayers at this time especially.

We as yet know nothing but what we have learned from the newspapers and we fear we never shall. Friday evening we saw in the journal that he was killed & Mr. [L.H.] *Boutell (my brother in law) left here Saturday evening for Poolesville spending the Sabbath in New York and arriving in Washington Monday morning. Meanwhile my brother Roger who was in New York started for Poolesville Saturday night where he arrived Sunday night. We have not yet heard the result of his investigations but Monday morning the news came that Evarts was among the missing so we have been in suspense ever since for there have been several different reports so that we can hardly believe anything. We have very little hope, however, that he is living:*

All this time Samuel has been away. He went to New York last week Wednesday and I thought that when he heard this news he would come home but Tuesday I received a letter from him & he had not heard anything about it evidently for he made no allusion to it. I immediately wrote him and I do hope he will come but as he is engaged to preach in Dr. Spring's church I do not know as he will come till Monday. It seems as if I must see him—I cannot bear to have him away at such a time.

He is wanted to preach in Dedham too next Sabbath.

Crosby came home yesterday on hearing of Evart's death and Marth is still here.

Tell Annie that I commenced a letter to her some time ago & that I will try to write soon but as present we are all very busy of course & I am too much excited to write much. My sister Mary is much better, she walked half a mile yesterday.

With much love & hoping soon to hear again from you I am as ever

Your affectionate daughter—Lizzie

Samuel considers himself quite well now & I think his trip to New York will do him good. I am very well with the exception of occasional headaches.

Appendix E

Letter from Private George H. Fernald

Company C, Second New York State Militia (Later Eighty-Second New York Infantry)

Camp Gorman

November 23, 1861

Cousin George,

Your most welcome letter of the 13th arrived at camp last Monday but as our company was out on picket, I did not receive it until last night. But I am glad to hear you are all well & enjoying good health.
You wanted to know if we had any men killed at the late battle. We had not. Our regiment did not cross at Conrad's Ferry where Baker's crossed at. We crossed at Edward's Ferry which is three miles below so we were not in the fight on the 21st of October but on the 22nd our company and Co. I of the [First] *Minnesota were out on picket when the rebel infantry of three thousand strong made a charge on us but out batteries opened on them which made great havoc among them. There was one man killed* [Lewis F. Mitchell of Co. I, First Minnesota Infantry] *& five wounded in the Minnesota Regiment but none in ours. But we had a tough time of it for it was cold & rainy all the time. We were there & we had nothing but our overcoats with us!*

I have not heard from sister in over a month but when I heard from her last, she was well.

You say you have plenty of rain in New York [City] *but we have a little more than a plenty here & cold rains at that too. And there is quite a difference in living in a warm house & a canvas tent. But I hope we will soon move farther south where it is warmer than it is here!*

But I must close now as I have to go out & drill so give my love to all the folks & keep a large share for yourself.

From your cousin, —George
P.S. Please excuse this as I wrote it in a hurry. —G.W.F.

George W. Fernald (1840–1918) resided in Orange County, New York, and enlisted on May 21, 1861, at age twenty-one to serve three years in Company C, Eighty-Second New York Volunteer Infantry. He was wounded in the chest at Gettysburg on July 3, 1863, and pronounced unfit for further service. He continued to serve as a payroll clerk in Baltimore until being mustered out of service in New York City on May 27, 1864.

Appendix F

The Belle of Amherst and Ball's Bluff

Herman Melville was not the only American writer to compose a poem creatively influenced by the Battle of Ball's Bluff. From her home in Amherst, Massachusetts, the reclusive Emily Dickinson was inspired by the losses suffered in the battle.

Dickinson, who wrote about half of her known poems during the Civil War, was moved by the deaths of several local soldiers. The poet contributed at least three poems to the daily journal *Drum Beat*, published from late February to early March 1864 to support the fundraising efforts of the Brooklyn and Long Island Sanitary Fair. *Drum Beat* was edited by an Amherst College graduate and Congregationalist minister, Richard Salter Storrs, who was an acquaintance of Dickinson's brother. Dickinson's Civil War poems, like much of her literary work, were never direct in their references. In a publication filled with boldly patriotic war rally verse and articles, Dickinson's poems are mysterious, artistic and complex. Indeed, Dickinson's observations about the war were moody and elliptical, conjuring a feeling rather than relying on literal reconstructions of historical events. In February 1863, Dickinson acknowledged the metaphorical nature of her work inspired by the conflict when she wrote to Colonel Thomas Wentworth Higginson that "war feels to me an oblique place."[248]

In her poem "When I Was Small, a Woman Died," likely composed during the years 1861–62, but not published until 1890, Dickinson reflects on the loss of a relative, Francis Howard Dickinson, who was killed in action at Ball's Bluff. The twenty-five-year-old Private Francis H. Dickinson enlisted in Company F, Fifteenth Massachusetts Volunteer Infantry, on July 12, 1861. Born in Belchertown, Massachusetts, he was employed as a blacksmith and living in Amherst when he joined the regiment. According to a history of the town published in 1896, Private Dickinson was "the first man on Amherst's quota to give up his life for his country." Dickinson was severely wounded at Ball's Bluff. On November 2, 1861, Worcester's weekly newspaper, the *Aegis & Transcript*, reported that Dickinson suffered the loss of "both legs shot off above the knee."[249]

In consecrating Private Dickinson's battlefield sacrifice, the poet envisioned a reunion of the soldier with his mother, who had died. Dickinson questioned whether "pride shall be in Paradise" but was unable to shake the image of loss. She wrote that the recurring image of the mother and her boy "Pass back and forth, before my Brain." The poet concludes her ode with the confidence that given the scale of war's sacrifice, there must be some resonating meaning to the loss—and presumably, to the war.

Notes

Introduction

1. Peirson, *Ball's Bluff*, 1.
2. Waugh, *Lincoln and McClellan*, 42.
3. Ibid., 44.
4. This interpretation is generally accepted by historians who have analyzed the period between the Manassas and Ball's Bluff battles, but an unpublished letter in a private collection suggests that the Confederates might have been contemplating an offensive movement just prior to the movements that resulted in the fight at Ball's Bluff. The letter, written in Confederate general Joseph E. Johnston's hand, is dated "Centreville, Virginia, October 23, 1861" and was directed to General P.G.T. Beauregard. It reads in part: "I have just received Col. Evans' note, of course the expedition talked of is dropped, but in view of the probability of the Colonel's surmise, that he may be attacked from the direction of Drainsville (*sic*), we had better keep twelve or fifteen regiments ready to move at a half hour's notice, upon the flank or rear of such an attacking force….Major Melton, who had charge of the prisoners for twelve or fifteen hours, says that they all concur in the report that their affair was part of a general plan – an attack all along the whole front. Perhaps they have fallen back at Leesburg because not ready elsewhere. It is to be hoped that at the next attempt the ploy may come off according to the programme…"

Chapter 1

5. Head, *History and Comprehensive Description*, 71–76.
6. Silverman, Thomas and Evans, *Shanks*, 28.
7. Harris, *Prison-Life*, 15.
8. Silverman, Thomas and Evans, *Shanks*, 76.
9. Ibid., 77.
10. Divine, *8th Virginia Infantry*, offers both a biographical sketch of Colonel Hunton as well as a full account of the regiment's service accompanied by a detailed roster.
11. Warner, *Generals in Gray*, 16.
12. Hess, *Field Armies*, 43. After the Battle of Ball's Bluff, there were a total of three forts, in addition to the masked battery, protecting Leesburg. Fort Evans, the largest of the forts, had been constructed before the battle and served as Colonel Evans's headquarters. Following the battle, Confederate general D.H. Hill ordered the construction of two other forts. Fort Johnson, named in honor of General Joseph E. Johnston, was built about two miles outside of town to the west, and Fort Beauregard was erected on a hill east of Leesburg. The historian Craig Swain conducted a detailed survey of Fort Evans. He noted that Fort Evans "was constructed on a knoll about 400 feet above sea level. The ground in front of the fort was a mix of broken ground descending to Goose Creek, about a mile and a half east, which flowed into the Potomac near Edward's Ferry." See www.markerhunter.wordpress.com.
13. Ibid.
14. Stiles, *Four Years*, 60.
15. Warner, *Generals in Blue*, 480.
16. Banes, *History*, 7–16. It may also be observed that the designation of the California regiments recruited in Pennsylvania was intended to solidify the bonds between the western state and the Union cause.
17. Holcombe, *First Minnesota*, 27.
18. Nielson, "Debacle at Ball's Bluff," 27.

Chapter 2

19. Waugh, *Lincoln and McClellan*, 49.
20. U.S. War Department, *Official Records* [hereafter *OR*], series 1, vol. 5, 587–88.
21. Ibid., 588.

22. Silverman, Thomas and Evans, *Shanks*, 78.
23. Ibid., 78.
24. *OR*, ser. 1, vol. 5, 591.
25. Patch, *Battle for Ball's Bluff*, 25–26; *OR*, ser. 1, vol. 5, 292.
26. Morgan, *Little Short of Boats*, 16.
27. Holien, "Battle of Ball's Bluff," 11.
28. *OR*, ser. 1, vol. 5, 347.
29. Morgan, *Little Short of Boats*, 19.
30. McClellan, *Reports and Campaigns*, 77.
31. *OR*, ser. 1, vol. 5, 290. McClellan failed to advise General Stone that McCall's force would not be remaining at Dranesville but had been ordered to return back to Langley. Absent that important information, Stone was under the impression that McCall's force was still holding a position around Dranesville and available for support when he initiated his own reconnaissance at Ball's Bluff.
32. Ibid., 293.
33. Miller, *Harvard's Civil War*, 55–56.
34. *OR*, ser. 1, vol. 5, 293.
35. Silverman, Thomas and Evans, *Shanks*, 81.
36. Diary of Private Albert Wymer Henley, see www.13thMississippi.com.
37. *OR*, ser. 1, vol. 5, 293.
38. Ibid., 293.
39. Root and JeStocker, *"Isn't This Glorious!"*, 200.
40. *OR*, ser. 1, vol. 5, 293–95.
41. Ibid., 293.
42. Ibid., 294. Lieutenant Church Howe also reported on the patrol, writing: "Our reconnaissance we were ordered to make toward Leesburg as far as we could do so safely, until we saw something to excite our suspicion.… We proceeded…three quarters of a mile or a mile from the edge of the river. We saw what we supposed to be an encampment. [There was] a row of maple trees; and there was a light on the opposite hill which shone through the trees and gave it the appearance of the camp. We were very well satisfied it was a camp." Quoted in Morgan, *Little Short of Boats*, 26.
43. Farwell, *Ball's Bluff*, 67.
44. *OR*, ser. 1, vol. 5, 294.
45. U.S. Congress, "Testimony of Colonel W.R. Lee," in *Report of the Committee on the Conduct of the War, Part Two* [hereafter CCW], 474.
46. Miller, *Harvard's Civil War*, 58–59.
47. Ibid., 59.

48. Ibid.
49. Winthrop, "Ball's Bluff," October 3, 1889.
50. *History of the Nineteenth*, 20
51. Bruce, *Twentieth Regiment*, 30–31.
52. *History of the Nineteenth*, 21.
53. *OR*, ser. 1, vol. 5, 308–9.
54. Ibid., 293.
55. Ibid., 294.
56. Ibid.
57. Ibid., 295.
58. Ward was a native of Worcester, Massachusetts, where he was employed as a machinist. At thirty-seven years old, Ward had served as a brigadier general in the state's prewar militia. He had been appointed lieutenant colonel of the Fifteenth Massachusetts on July 24, 1861. According to one soldier, Ward was regarded as "a stern disciplinarian, if not severe," Root and Stocker, *"Isn't It Glorious!,"* 5.
59. See *Colonel Edward D. Baker: Lincoln's Constant Ally* by Harry C. Blair and Rebecca Tarshis for more details on Baker's life.
60. Burlingame and Ettlinger, *Inside Lincoln's White House*, 285.
61. *OR*, ser. 1, vol. 5, 295.
62. CCW, "Testimony of General Stone," 277.
63. Ibid., 303.

Chapter 3

64. Patch, *Battle for Ball's Bluff*, 71.
65. Miller, *Harvard Regiment*, 23.
66. Root and Stocker, "*Isn't it Glorious!*," 200.
67. Bruce, *Twentieth Massachusetts*, 31.
68. Morgan, *Ball's Bluff*, 35.
69. Bruce, *Twentieth Massachusetts*, 32; *OR*, ser. 1, vol. 5, 309.
70. Report of Captain Lorenzo D. Fletcher, see www.13thMississippiInfantry.com.
71. *National Tribune*, March 15, 1894.
72. CCW, "Testimony of Charles Devens," 403–12.
73. Scott, *Fallen Leaves*, 67.
74. *OR*, ser. 1, vol. 5, 33.
75. Ibid., 499.

76. Ibid., 310.
77. Ibid., 294.
78. *National Tribune*, March 15, 1894.
79. Patch, *Battle for Ball's Bluff*, 78–79.
80. Scott, *Fallen Leaves*, 62.
81. *OR*, ser. 1, vol. 5, 320–23.
82. *History of the Nineteenth*, 22.
83. *OR*, ser. 1, vol. 5, 303.
84. Ibid., 502.
85. Ibid., 333–34.
86. Farwell, *Ball's Bluff*, 86–87.
87. Ibid., 87.

Chapter 4

88. Miller, *Harvard's Civil War*, 65.
89. CCW, 408.
90. Ballard, *Battle of Ball's Bluff*, 22.
91. Scott, *Fallen Leaves*, 62.
92. CCW, 408.
93. Ballard, *Battle of Ball's Bluff*, 24.
94. Bailey, *Forward to Richmond*, 45. The actual quote from Sir Walter Scott's 1810 lyric poem *The Lady of the Lake* reads: "One blast upon his bugle-horn/Were worth a thousand men" from canto 6, stanza 18.
95. CCW, Testimony of Lieutenant Colonel Wistar, 308.
96. *Hartford Weekly Times*, November 2, 1861.
97. CCW, Testimony of Lieutenant Colonel Wistar, 309.
98. Report of Captain Lorenzo D. Fletcher, see www.13thMississippiInfantry.com.
99. *History of the Nineteenth*, 22–23.
100. *OR*, ser. 1, vol. 5, 376.
101. Ibid., 371.
102. Wheelock, "When Green Wore Blue," 24–31.
103. Sack, "In Search of Colonel Ward."
104. Howe, *Touched with Fire*, 13–19.
105. Novick, *Honorable Justice*, 49.
106. *Local News* (Alexandria, VA), December 30, 1861.
107. Scott, *Fallen Leaves*, 62.

108. Palfrey, *Memoir*, 23–24.
109. Caspar Crowinshield to Harriet Sears Crowinshield, October 22, 1861, Charles Pickering Putnam Papers, Massachusetts Historical Society.
110. Bruce, *Twentieth Regiment*, 48.
111. Miller, *Harvard's Civil War*, 72.
112. Morgan, *Ball's Bluff*, offers an extensive essay about the various accounts of Baker's death, 223–31.
113. *Hartford Weekly Times*, November 2, 1861.
114. *National Tribune*, October 3, 1889.
115. Crowinshield letter, Massachusetts Historical Society.
116. Morgan, *Ball's Bluff*, 230.
117. *National Tribune*, October 3, 1889.
118. Morgan, *Ball's Bluff*, 139.
119. *OR*, ser. 1, vol. 5, 328. Captain Louis Bieral (who also went by the name Lewis Clark) was a native of Chile who had gone to California for the gold rush. He was forced to flee the rough-and-tumble California frontier after being convicted of shooting a prostitute. He was described as "black-haired with a flowing mustache and of a stout, muscular body" that was tattooed from head to foot. He had a checkered career before the Civil War (including charges that he had killed his mistress in Boston) that failed to settle after the war. Regarded as a hero of Ball's Bluff, he resigned his commission on April 12, 1862, due to poor health. After several years of gambling, saloon keeping and small criminal enterprises, Bieral secured a position as a customs inspector in New York. He remained in the post for nearly twenty years until he was dismissed from his post for demanding bribes. On November 1, 1886, Bieral entered the office of Hans Beattie, the surveyor of the Port of New York, and fired two pistol shots at his former boss. Beattie survived his wounds, and New York was treated to a sensational trial that was covered by all of the major newspapers. One of Bieral's attorneys in the matter was the controversial former Union general Daniel E. Sickles. Bieral was convicted of assault with intent to kill and sentenced to five years at Auburn Prison. He was pardoned in 1890. See *New York Times*, January 27, 1887, and Andrew Wender Cohen's *Contraband: Smuggling and the Birth of the American Century*.
120. *Hartford Weekly Times*, November 2, 1861.
121. *History of the Nineteenth Regiment*, 22.
122. *National Tribune*, October 3, 1889.
123. *History of the Nineteenth Regiment*, 22.
124. *OR*, ser. 1, vol. 5, 499.

Chapter 5

125. *OR*, ser. 1, vol. 5, 310.
126. Morgan, *Little Short of Boats*, 141. Colonel Cogswell was later presented with an ornamental Tiffany sword by the City of New York. On one side of the blade was etched his rallying cry at Ball's Bluff: "Boys, we'll cut our way through to Edward's Ferry." This sword remains in the possession of Cogswell's descendants.
127. *National Tribune*, July 20, 1893
128. Wexler, *Tammany Regiment*, 47–48.
129. *OR*, ser. 1, vol. 5, 311.
130. It is clear from Colonel Cogswell's official report dated September 22, 1862, that he is the officer Colonel Devens referred to in his report, see *OR*, ser. 1, vol. 5, 322. It should be noted that, of the recent published studies of the Battle, Byron Farwell's *Ball's Bluff* (106–8) is the only work that accurately analyzes Cogswell's report and places it within its proper historical context. Captain Charles Eager claimed in an article written for the *National Tribune* in 1894 that the identity of the "mysterious officer" was none other than Elijah V. White. He said that a delegation of veterans from the Fifteenth Massachusetts met White, who was then living in Leesburg in 1886, and that White told them he had shouted "Come on, boys!" and the Yankees rushed toward him and received a terrible fire.
131. *OR*, ser. 1, vol. 5, 322.
132. Morgan, *Little Short of Boats*, 143.
133. Undated newspaper clipping in scrapbook of the Forty-Second New York Volunteer Infantry, New York State Division of Military and Naval Affairs.
134. Morgan, *Little Short of Boats*, 143.
135. *OR*, ser. 1, vol. 5, 361.
136. Scott, *Fallen Leaves*, 63.
137. Hamilton, *Papers*, vol. 1, 118. It should be noted that the local historian John Divine, who was a great student of the Ball's Bluff battle and Loudoun County history, always tried to temper historical reliance on the Shotwell papers, as he viewed them as more fiction than fact.
138. Hanaford, *Young Captain*, 104.
139. Letters from Henry M. Tremlett, Reports, Letters and Papers Appertaining to Twentieth Massachusetts Volunteer Infantry, by Association of Officers of the Twentieth Massachusetts Volunteer Infantry (Boston: Boston Public Library, 1905), 168.

140. Letter from Sergeant Walter A. Eames, Company B, Fifteenth Massachusetts Volunteer Infantry, to his wife, Poolesville, Maryland, October 22, 1861, private collection.
141. Letter from Lieutenant Charles H. Eager, Fifteenth Massachusetts Volunteer Infantry, to his wife, Poolesville, Maryland, October 22, 1861, private collection.
142. *History of the Nineteenth Massachusetts*, 22–23.
143. Undated newspaper clipping in the scrapbook of the Forty-Second New York Volunteer Infantry, New York State Division of Military and Naval Affairs. Timothy O'Meara was also listed on muster rolls as "O'Mara." He was born in Tipperary, Ireland, and enrolled in the Forty-Second New York Infantry at Great Neck, New York, on May 3, 1861. He was twenty-six years old. He had come to the United States in 1855 and served in Mexico with Juarez's forces in the Mexican Revolution. After his capture at Ball's Bluff, he was made a prisoner of war and incarcerated at the Liggon Tobacco Warehouse in Richmond. He was exchanged for a Confederate soldier being held by Union forces on September 21, 1862. American Civil War Database, accessed February 8, 2017, http://civilwardata.com/active/hdsquery.dll?SoldierHistory?U&15365583. During his imprisonment, O'Meara befriended Colonel Michael Corcoran of the Irish Brigade. Corcoran helped him secure a colonel's commission in a new Irish regiment that was being raised, the Ninetieth Illinois Infantry. O'Meara was leading that unit when he was mortally wounded in November 1863. For more, see James B. Swan, *Chicago's Irish Legion: The 90th Illinois Volunteers in the Civil War* (Carbondale: Southern Illinois University Press, 2009), 17–18.

The story of Captain Michael Garetty did not end with the stirring published accounts of his heroism. In November 1861, a flag of truce was agreed to allow a number of New York officers to retrieve the body of Captain Henry Alden, who was killed at Ball's Bluff and had been buried on the field. The details of the recovery of Captain Alden's body and its return to his family were reported in a *New York Times* article. The account of the recovery of Captain Alden's remains generated numerous requests from the relatives of others slain in the battle to similarly retrieve the bodies of their loved ones. General Stone refused such requests and denied parties visiting the front for such purpose to travel over to the Ball's Bluff battlefield. One of these requests came from the widow of Captain Garetty. After General Stone refused to allow for the recovery of Captain Garetty's remains, his widow returned to New York. On January 9, 1862, a letter titled "A Woman's Story" was published in the *New York Tribune*. It was signed, "A Soldier's Mother," but was clearly written by those intent on trying to recover Captain Garetty's remains. The letter was intended to embarrass General Stone and help fan the flames of disloyal conspiracy that were already encircling him. The day after the letter appeared, a letter was published in the *New York Times* defending General Stone and countering many of the charges that were leveled against him in the *Tribune* letter. It was strongly suggested by the author of the *Tribune* letter, who purportedly witnessed the civil personal exchange between General Stone and Garetty's widow at Stone's Poolesville, Maryland headquarters, that Mrs. Garetty was being used to cast aspersions on the service of Stone as part of the effort to question his loyalty to the Union cause. Wexler, *Tammany Regiment*, 53–55.

144. Palfrey, *Memoir for William Francis Bartlett*, 25–26.
145. Morgan, *Little Short of Boats*, 224–25. An article published in the *Confederate Veteran* magazine in 1898 claimed that it was Sergeant Hatcher who "ran out of the line and fired the fatal shot" that killed Colonel Baker. Later historians have repeated variations of this story (see Farwell, *Ball's Bluff*, 102) but the tale was dismissed by several witnesses, including Lieutenant Henry Abbott of the Twentieth Massachusetts. The late Loudoun County historian John Divine questioned the origins of the story of the Hatcher monument and attributed it to later tourism visits to the battlefield. Still, the monument is composed of New England granite.
146. Bruce, *Twentieth Massachusetts*, 56–57.
147. *OR*, ser. 1, vol. 5, 318-320.
148. Letters from Henry Tremlett, 168.
149. *Boston Journal*, October 26, 1861.
150. Ballard, *Battle of Ball's Bluff*, 34.
151. *Military Images*, "Faces of Ball's Bluff," Spring 2017.
152. Peirson, *Ball's Bluff*, 5.
153. Undated newspaper clipping in the scrapbook of the Forty-Second New York Volunteer Infantry, New York State Division of Military and Naval Affairs.
154. Bruce, *Twentieth Massachusetts*, 53–54.
155. *The World*, November 2, 1861.
156. Bailey, *Civil War*, 51.
157. *History of the Nineteenth Massachusetts*, 25.
158. Swan, *Chicago's Irish Legion*, 17–18.
159. *OR*, ser. 1, vol. 5, 312–14.

160. Ibid.
161. Wexler, *Tammany Regiment*, 57–58.
162. *OR*, ser. 1, vol. 5, 325.
163. James A. Morgan III, "Ball's Bluff: "A Very Nice Little Military Chance," in *Civil War in Loudon County*, edited by Stephen F. Meserve, 41.
164. It is difficult to definitively ascertain the casualties of Ball's Bluff. A revised table, reflecting research in original muster rolls, regimental histories and other source materials, is included in Appendix A (Tables 1 and 2). The roster (see Appendix B) of Union soldiers killed in the Ball's Bluff fight includes the names of those who were wounded and died in the months following the battle. The wounded suffered severely, and the names of these soldiers should be included among those who lost their lives on the field of battle.
165. Harris, *Prison-Life in the Tobacco Warehouse*, 14.
166. Peirson, *Ball's Bluff*, 6.
167. Wexler, *Tammany Regiment*, 68.
168. Jeffrey, *Richmond Prisons*, 38–39.
169. Ibid., 41. Congressman Alfred Ely, who had been taken prisoner during the Union rout at the First Battle of Bull Run, made the selections. In his journal, he related the tense scene: "[Colonel Lee] read the name on each paper [and] folded it and placed it in a tin tube nearly a foot long and only large enough to admit the hand. After shaking up the ballots, General Winder requested me to to draw from the case a ballot and the Colonel whose name was drawn would be the one who would stand as hostage for the privateer Smith, now condemned to death in Philadelphia. This I declined to do except at the instance and request of the officers. The unpleasant duty, so suddenly imposed on me in presence of the deeply interested array of military men, produced a most thrilling feeling of regret and pain; and I would gladly have been spared the unwelcome task, called upon as I was to draw lots for one among the six brave and gallant officers who had fought the battles of his country, and who would have removed from his comparatively comfortable quarters to a felon's dungeon; there to suffer and stand as a pledge to die in case of the execution of a condemned pirate."
170. Root and Stocker, *"Isn't This Glorious!,"* 93.

Chapter 6

171. Oates, *With Malice Toward None*, 264.
172. Blair and Tarshis, *Lincoln's Constant Ally*, 133.
173. Oates, *With Malice Toward None*, 284.
174. Ibid., 285.
175. Sears, *Civil War Papers*, 110. Shortly after sending this dispatch to General Stone, McClellan telegraphed General N.P. Banks: "Push forward your command as rapidly as possible and put as many men over the river to reinforce Genl. Stone as you can before daylight. Genl. Stone is directed to hold his command on the Virginia side of the Potomac at all hazards and informed that you will support him. You will assume command when you join General Stone."
176. *OR*, ser. 1, vol. 5, 367.
177. Holien, *Battle of Ball's Bluff*, 82.
178. CCW, 295.
179. Ibid..
180. Quoted in Holien, *Battle of Ball's Bluff*, 82.
181. Ballard, *Battle of Ball's Bluff*, 36.
182. Sears, *Civil War*, 111. On October 25, 1861, McClellan wrote to his wife from Washington: "The man directly to blame for the affair was Col. Baker who was killed—he was in command, disregarded entirely the instructions he had received from Stone & violated all military rules & precautions. Instead of meeting the enemy with double their force & a good ferry behind him, he was outnumbered three to one, & had no means of retreat."
183. Ibid.

Chapter 7

184. Ball's Bluff seemed a significant battle in the autumn of 1861, but later battles would overshadow the military aspects of the fight. In 1866, General Stone wrote that Ball's Bluff was such a minor affair "about equal to an unnoticed morning's skirmish on the lines before Petersburg at a later period in the war." (Morgan/Meserve, *Civil War in Loudon County*, 42). The Union brigadier general Alpheus Williams attributed caution on the part of the Union command structure to the legacy of the battle, writing: "That cursed Ball's Bluff haunts the souls of our chiefs." (Morgan, *Little Short of Boats*, 193).

185. Tap, *Over Lincoln's Shoulder*, 22.
186. Ibid.
187. Long, "True Believers," 21.
188. Ibid., 22.
189. Beard, "Scapegoat of Ball's Bluff."
190. Ibid.
191. Tap, "Amateurs at War," 1.
192. Sears, *Lincoln's Lieutenants*, 131.
193. *New York Times*, March 3, 1862.
194. Ecelbarger, *Frederick W. Lander*, 149. Little-known today, Frederick Lander (1822–1862) was an American original. Lander made almost annual explorations of the central western plains during the years 1853 and 1860. Lander's well-documented Oregon Trail expedition of 1859 helped to establish the reputation of the great landscape artist Albert Bierstadt, who was among several artists Lander recruited for his expedition. Lander was well known for his personal bravery, engaging in a slugfest with a political opponent at Willard's Hotel in Washington in 1859 that received national press coverage. He also offered himself as a substitute for Wisconsin congressman John F. Potter in a duel that had been offered to Potter by the Southern representative Roger Pryor over words exchanged on the congressional floor. Lander selected Bowie knives as the weapon of choice, and the diminutive Pryor wisely noted that he had no issue of honor with Lander. Such actions gained the attention and respect of General George B. McClellan and Secretary of War Edwin Stanton. (Houston and Houston, "1859 Lander Expedition Revisited.") In announcing Lander's death, the *New York Times* wrote: "In person he was tall, stalwart, graceful and proud, and, mounted on his charger and in his fine military costume, he looked like a knight of olden times. In his loss, the country loses one of its best men and soldiers, and the tears of his command and nation, follow him to the grave." (*New York Times*, March 3, 1862).
195. CCW, 260.
196. Tap, *Over Lincoln's Shoulder*, 66.
197. Beard, "Scapegoat of Ball's Bluff." The term "Team of Rivals" served as the title of historian Doris Kearns Goodwin's award-winning biography of Abraham Lincoln. Goodwin argued that Lincoln had eased tensions in the North by bringing many of his leading political opponents into his administration.
198. Beard, "Scapegoat of Ball's Bluff."

199. See CCW testimony of Lieutenant Philip J. Downey, Company I, Second New York State Militia, 300. Lieutenant Downey testified before the Committee on the Conduct of the War on January 10, 1862, regarding mysterious letters and dispatches that passed between General Stone and the Virginia shore. When asked by Congressman Covode as to the general feeling among the soldiers toward General Stone, Lieutenant Downey responded: "The general feeling is that a great portion of the officers and men do not think he is altogether on the square."
200. Sears, *Lincoln's Lieutenants*, 142.
201. CCW, 306.
202. Lamb, *Extraordinary Life*, 121.
203. Morgan, *Little Short of Boats*, 198.
204. Lamb, *Extraordinary Life*, 148.

Chapter 8

205. Irwin, "Ball's Bluff," 133.
206. Tap, *Over Lincoln's Shoulder*, 69.
207. Ibid.
208. Ibid.
209. Irwin, "Ball's Bluff," 137.
210. CCW, 134.
211. CCW, 429.
212. Sears, *George B. McClellan*, 145–46.
213. Lamb, *Life of Charles Pomeroy Stone*, 157.
214. Ibid., 158.
215. Sears, *Civil War Papers*, 146
216. Morgan, *Little Short of Boats*, 202.
217. Lamb, *Life of Charles Pomeroy Stone*, 152.
218. Morgan, *Little Short of Boats*, 202.
219. Farwell, *Ball's Bluff*, 216.
220. Letter from Private Solomon B. Clark, Company I, Thirty-Fourth New York Volunteer Infantry, from Poolesville, Maryland, February 15, 1862, in the author's collection. The Thirty-Fourth New York Infantry was known as a regiment strongly loyal to General McClellan. When the unit completed its term of two years of service, it returned to Albany and paraded up State Street carrying a framed portrait of McClellan. A contemporary newspaper account reported: "As with all the other

returned regiments McClellan is their idol, and they avail themselves of every opportunity to testify to their unbounded admiration of him." The Thirty-Fourth New York had left for war counting over 800 men but came home with only 427 left in the ranks. Private Clark did not return. Just three months after writing this letter, he was mortally wounded on June 1, 1862, at the Battle of Fair Oaks, Virginia.

221. Ibid., 217.
222. Lamb, *Life of Charles Pomeroy Stone*, 163.
223. Ibid., 163–65.
224. *National Republican*, April 10, 1863.
225. Marvel, *Lincoln's Autocrat*, 224.
226. Ibid., 225.
227. *National Republican*, April 10, 1863.
228. Sears, *Lincoln's Lieutenants*, 144
229. Morgan, *Little Short of Boats*, 203.
230. Lamb, *Life of Charles Pomeroy Stone*, 173.
231. Morgan, *Little Short of Boats*, 203.
232. Ibid..
233. Ibid., 206.

Chapter 9

234. *New York Times*, April 27, 1862.
235. Pennsylvania, *Reports of the Heads of Departments*, 4.
236. *New York World*, November 2, 1861.
237. *Ibid.*
238. Scott, *Fallen Leaves*, 60.
239. Peirson, *Ball's Bluff*, 7.
240. *Harper's Weekly*, November 9, 1861.
241. Government Printing Office, Letter of the Secretary of War, Transmitting the Report on the Organization of the Army of the Potomac and of its Campaigns in Virginia and Maryland, Under the Command of Maj. Gen. George B. McClellan, from July 26, 1861 to November 7, 1862 (Washington, 1864), 32.
242. Ibid., 32.
243. Ibid., 35.
244. Letter from Private Theodore G. Goff, Company G, Fifth Connecticut Volunteer Infantry to his mother, Mrs. William Gay, dated March 17,

1862, in the author's collection. Goff enlisted in the Fifth Connecticut Infantry on September 12, 1861. Promoted to corporal in 1862, he survived the war and was mustered out of service in July 1865.
245. Novick, *Honorable Justice*, 52–53.
246. Divine, *8th Virginia Infantry*, 7.
247. Cohen, *Selected Poems*.

Appendix F

248. https://www.emilydickinsonmuseum.org/civilwar.
249. *Worcester Aegis & Transcript*, November 2, 1861, Vol. 24, 41.

Bibliography

Association of Officers of the Twentieth Massachusetts Volunteer Infantry. *Reports, Letters & Papers Appertaining to the 20th Mass. Vol. Inf.* Boston: Boston Public Library Rare Books Collection, n.d.

Bailey, Ronald H. *The Civil War: Forward to Richmond, McClellan's Peninsular Campaign*. Alexandria, VA: Time-Life Books, 1983.

Ballard, Ted. *Battle of Ball's Bluff: Staff Ride Guide*. Washington, D.C.: Center of Military History, 2001.

Baltz, John D. *Colonel E.D. Baker's Defense in the Battle of Ball's Bluff, Fought October 21st 1861 in Virginia and Slight Biographical Sketches of Colonel Baker and Generals Wistar and Stone*. Lancaster, PA: Inquirer Printing Company, 1888.

Banes, Charles H. *History of the Philadelphia Brigade*. Philadelphia: J.B. Lippincott, 1876.

Basler, Roy P. *The Collected Works of Abraham Lincoln*. New Brunswick, NJ: Rutgers University Press, 1953.

Beard, Rick. "The Scapegoat of Ball's Bluff." *New York Times*, January 15, 2012.

Blair, Harry C., and Rebecca Tarshis. *Lincoln's Constant Ally: The Life of Colonel Edward D. Baker*. Portland: Oregon Historical Society, 1960.

Boatner, Mark M. *The Civil War Dictionary*. New York: David McKay, 1959.

Bruce, George A. *The Twentieth Regiment of Massachusetts Volunteer Infantry 1861–1865*. Boston: Houghton Mifflin Company, 1906.

Buel, Clarence C., and Robert Underwood Johnson, eds. *Battles and Leaders of the Civil War*. Vol. 2. New York: Century Company, 1887.

Burlingame, Michael, and John R. Turner Ettlinger. *Inside Lincoln's White House: The Complete Civil War Diary of John Hay*. Carbondale: Southern Illinois University Press, 1997.

Catton, Bruce. *The Army of the Potomac: Mr. Lincoln's Army.* Garden City, NY: Doubleday, 1951.

Clark, Private Solomon B. Letter dated February 15, 1862, from Poolesville, Maryland to "Friends at Home." Author's collection.

Cohen, Andrew Wender. *Contraband: Smuggling and the Birth of the American Century*. New York: W.W. Norton, 2015.

Cohen, Henig, ed. *Selected Poems of Herman Melville.* Garden City, NY: Doubleday, 1964.

Conkling, Arthur R. *The Life and Letters of Roscoe Conkling.* New York: Charles L. Webster, 1889.

Conkling, Roscoe. *Privileges of the House of Representatives. Battle of Ball's Bluff. Speech of Hon. Roscoe Conkling of New York Delivered in the House of Representatives, January 6, 1982.* Washington, D.C.: Scammel & Company, 1862.

Daily Journal Evansville (IN). February 13, 1862.

Devens, Arthur, Lithgow, ed. *Charles Devens' Orations and Addresses.* Boston: Little, Brown & Company, 1891.

Divine, John E. *8th Virginia Infantry*. Lynchburg, VA: H.E. Howard Inc., 1984.

Ecelbarger, Gary L. *Frederick W. Lander: The Great Natural American Soldier*. Baton Rouge: Louisiana State University Press, 2001.

Farwell, Byron. *Ball's Bluff: A Small Battle and Its Long Shadow.* McLean, VA: EPM Publications Inc., 1990.

Ford, Andrew E. *The Story of the 15th Regiment Massachusetts Volunteer Infantry in the Civil War.* Clinton, MA: W.J. Coulter, 1898.

Ford, Worthington Chauncey, ed. *A Cycle of Adams Letters 1861–1865*. Boston: Houghton Mifflin Company, 1920.

Goff, Private Theodore G. Letter to his mother dated March 17, 1862. Author's collection.

Goodheart, Adam. *1861: The Civil War Awakening*. New York: Alfred A. Knopf, 2011.

Grimsely, Mark. "The Definition of Disaster." *Civil War Times Illustrated* (May 1989).

Hamilton, J.G. De Roulhac ed. *The Papers of Randolph Abbott Shotwell.* Vol 1. Raleigh: North Carolina Historical Commission, 1929.

Hanaford, P.A. *The Young Captain: A Memorial of Capt. Richard C. Derby.* Boston: Degen, Estes & Company, 1865.

Harper's Weekly (New York). November 9, 1861.

Harris, Lieutenant William C. *Prison-Life in the Tobacco Warehouse at Richmond by a Ball's Bluff Prisoner*. Philadelphia: George H. Childs, 1862.

Hassler, Warren W. *General George B. McClellan: Shield of the Union*. Westport, CT: Greenwood Press Publishers, 1974.

Head, James W. *History and Comprehensive Description of Loudoun County Virginia*. Leesburg, VA: Park View Press, 1908.

Hess, Earl J. *Field Armies & Fortifications in the Civil War: The Eastern Campaigns*. Chapel Hill: University of North Carolina Press, 2005.

Hesseltine, William B., and Hazel C. Wolf. *The Blue and the Gray on the Nile*. Chicago: University of Chicago Press, 1961.

Hillard, G.S. *Life and Campaigns of George B. McClellan*. Philadelphia: J.B. Lippincott, 1864.

History of the Nineteenth Regiment Massachusetts Volunteer Infantry 1861–1865. Salem, MA: Salem Press, 1906.

Holcombe, R.I. *The First Minnesota Volunteer Infantry 1861–1864*. Stillwater, MN: Easton & Masterman, 1916.

Holien, Kim Bernard. *Battle of Ball's Bluff*. Orange, VA: Moss Publications, 1985.

———. "The Battle of Ball's Bluff, October 21, 1861." *Blue & Gray Magazine* 7, no. 3 (February 1990).

Houston, Alan Fraser, and Jourdon Moore Houston. "The 1859 Lander Expedition Revisited: Worthy Relics Tell New Tales of a Wind River Wagon Road." *Montana: The Magazine of Western History* (Summer 1999): 50–71.

Howard, William F. *The Battle of Ball's Bluff: "The Leesburg Affair, October 21, 1861."* Lynchburg: H.E. Howard Inc., 1994.

———. "Disaster at Ball's Bluff: Another Union Defeat Leaves Lincoln on the Defensive." *Albany Times Union*, October 16, 2011.

Howe, Mark De Wolfe. *Touched with Fire: Civil War Letters and Diary of Oliver Wendell Holmes 1861–1864*. Cambridge, MA: Harvard University Press, 1946.

Imholite, John Quinn. *The First Volunteers: History of the First Minnesota Volunteer Regiment 1861–1865*. Minneapolis, MN: Ross & Haines Inc., 1963.

Irwin, Lieutenant Colonel Richard B. "Ball's Bluff and the Arrest of General Stone." In *Battles and Leaders of the Civil War*, edited by Clarence C. Buel and Robert U. Johnson. Vol. 2, 123–34. New York: Century Company, 1884, 1887, 1888.

Jeffrey, William H. *Richmond Prisons 1861–1862*. St. Johnsbury, VT: The Republican Press, 1893.

Lamb, Blaine. *The Extraordinary Life of Charles Pomeroy Stone, Soldier, Surveyor, Pasha, Engineer*. Yardley, PA: Westholme Publishing, 2015.

Lash, Gary G. *"Duty Well Done": The History of Edward Baker's California Regiment (71st Pennsylvania Infantry)*. Baltimore: Butternut and Blue, 2001.

Leech, Margaret. *Reveille in Washington*. New York: Harper and Brothers, 1941.

Letter of the Secretary of War, Transmitting Report on the Organization of the Army of the Potomac, and of its Campaigns in Virginia and Maryland, Under the Command of Maj. Gen. George B. McClellan, from July 26, 1861, to November 7, 1862. Washington, D.C.: Government Printing Office, 1864.

Local News (Alexandria, VA). December 1861.

Long, E.B. "The True Believers: The Committee on the Conduct of the War." *Civil War Times Illustrated* (August 1981).

Marvel, William. *Lincoln's Autocrat: The Life of Edwin Stanton*. Chapel Hill: University of North Carolina Press, 2015.

McClellan, George B. *General McClellan's Reports and Campaigns*. New York: Sheldon and Company, 1864.

———. *McClellan's Own Story*. New York: Charles L. Webster, 1887.

McLean, Jess N., ed. *The Official Records of the 13th Mississippi Regiment…as Told by Those Who Were There*. Privately published, 2012.

Meserve, Stephen F., ed. *The Civil War in Loudon County, Virginia: A History of Hard Times*. Charleston, SC: The History Press, 2008.

Military Images. "Faces of Ball's Bluff." Spring 2017.

Miller, Richard F. "Brahmins Under Fire: Peer Courage and the Harvard Regiment." *Historical Journal of Massachusetts* 30, no. 1 (Winter 2002). Retrieved from HJM's online archive at http:www.westfield.ma.edu/mhj.

———. *Harvard's Civil War: A History of the Twentieth Massachusetts Volunteer Infantry*. Hanover, NH: University Press of New England, 2005.

Mitchell, Lieutenant Colonel Joseph B. "Debacle at Ball's Bluff." *Civil War Times* (January 1962).

Morgan, James III. "Ball's Bluff: "A Very Nice Little Military Chance." In *The Civil War in Loudon County, Virginia: A History of Hard Times*, by Stephen F. Meserve. Charleston, SC: The History Press, 2008.

———. *A Little Short of Boats: The Battles of Ball's Bluff & Edwards Ferry, October 21–22, 1861*. New York: Savas Beatie, 2011.

National Republican (Washington, D.C.). April 10, 1863.

National Tribune (Washington, D.C.). 1893–1894.

New York Times. 1861–1862.

New York World. November 2, 1861.

Nichols, Edward J. *Toward Gettysburg: A Biography of General John F. Reynolds.* University Park: Pennsylvania State University Press, 1958.

Nielson, Jon M., ed. "Debacle at Ball's Bluff." *Civil War Times Illustrated* (January 1976).

Novick, Sheldon M. *Honorable Justice: The Life of Oliver Wendell Holmes.* New York: Dell Publishing, 1989.

Oates, Stephen B. *With Malice Toward None: The Life of Abraham Lincoln.* New York: Harper & Row Publishers, 1977.

Palfrey, Francis Winthrop. *Memoir for William Francis Bartlett.* Boston: Houghton, Osgood & Company, 1878.

Patch, Joseph D. *The Battle for Ball's Bluff.* Leesburg, VA: Potomac Press, 1958.

Peirson, Charles L. *Ball's Bluff; An Episode and Its Consequences to Some of Us, A Paper Written for the Military History Society of Massachusetts.* Salem, MA: Salem Press, 1913.

Pennsylvania, State of. *Reports of the Heads of Departments, Transmitted to the Governor of Pennsylvania in Pursuance of Law for the Financial Year Ending Nov. 30, 1862.* Harrisburg, PA: Singerly & Myers, 1863.

Ramey, Emily, and John K. Gott, eds. *The Years of Anguish: Fauquier County, Virginia 1861–1865.* Fauquier County Civil War Centennial Committee, 1959.

Report of the Committee on the Conduct of the War. Part Two. Washington, D.C.: U.S. Government Printing Office, 1863.

Root, Edwin R., and Jeffrey D. Stocker. *"Isn't This Glorious!" The 15th, 19th and 20th Massachusetts Volunteer Infantry Regiments at Gettysburg's Copse of Trees.* Bethlehem, PA: Moon Trail Books, 2006.

Ropes, John Codman, and Florian Dexheimer, eds. *Right Up into the Fire: The Civil War Letters of Lieutenant Henry Ropes, 20th Massachusetts Volunteer Infantry.* Privately printed, 2017.

Sack, Pamela H. "In Search of Colonel Ward." Telegram.com, August 23, 2013.

Sears, Stephen W., ed. *The Civil War Papers of George B. McClellan: Selected Correspondence 1860–1865.* New York: Ticknor & Fields, 1989.

———. *George B. McClellan: The Young Napoleon.* New York: Ticknor & Fields, 1988.

———. *Lincoln's Lieutenants: The High Command of the Army of the Potomac.* Boston: Houghton Mifflin Harcourt, 2017.

Scott, Robert Garth, ed. *Fallen Leaves: The Civil War Letters of Major Henry Livermore Abbott.* Kent, OH: Kent State University Press, 1991.

Silverman, Jason H., Samuel N. Thomas and Beverly D. Evans IV. *Shanks: The Life and Wars of General Nathan G. Evans, CSA*. Cambridge, MA: Da Capo, 2002.

Stahr, Walter. *Stanton: Lincoln's War Secretary*. New York: Simon & Schuster, 2017.

Stiles, Robert. *Four Years Under Marse Robert.* New York: Neale Publishing Company, 1903.

Stowe, Sergeant Jonathan P. "Life with the 15th Massachusetts." *Civil War Times Illustrated* (August 1972).

Swan, James B. *Chicago's Irish Legion: The 90th Illinois Volunteers in the Civil War.* Carbondale: Southern Illinois University Press, 2009.

Tap, Bruce. "Amateurs at War: Abraham Lincoln and the Committee on the Conduct of the War." *Journal of the Abraham Lincoln Association* 23, no. 2 (Summer 2002): 1–18.

———. *Over Lincoln's Shoulder: The Committee on the Conduct of the War*. Lawrence: University Press of Kansas, 1998.

U.S. Congress. *Report of the Committee on the Conduct of the War, Part Two*. Washington, D.C.: U.S. Government Printing Office, 1863.

U.S. War Department. *Official Records of the War of the Rebellion.* Washington, D.C.: U.S. Government Printing Office, 1894.

Warner, Ezra. *Generals in Blue: Lives of the Union Commanders.* Baton Rouge: Louisiana State University Press, 1959.

———. *Generals in Gray: Lives of the Confederate Commanders.* Baton Rouge: Louisiana State University Press, 1959.

Waugh, John C. *Lincoln and McClellan: The Troubled Partnership Between a President and His General*. New York: Palgrave MacMillan, 2010.

Wexler, Fred C. *The Tammany Regiment: A History of the Forty-Second New York Volunteer Infantry 1861–1864*. Bloomington: iUniverse, 2016.

Wheelock, Dr. Seymour E. "When Green Wore Blue." *Dartmouth Medicine* (Spring 1993): 24–31.

Wilkes, George. *McClellan: From Ball's Bluff to Antietam*. New York: Sinclair Tousey, 1863.

Winthrop, Thomas F. "Ball's Bluff: One of the First Great Mistakes of the War." *National Tribune*, October 3, 1889.

Wistar, Isaac J. *Autobiography of Isaac Jones Wistar, 1827–1905.* Philadelphia: Wistar Institute of Anatomy and Biology, 1937.

Index

D

E

F

G

H

I

J

K

L

M

U

V

W

Y

About the Author

Bill Howard is a New York–based author and historian who has published numerous books and articles about military and social history. Howard graduated from Manhattanville College (BA, 1983) with a degree in American Studies and was a Herbert H. Lehman Fellow at the University at Albany Graduate School of Public Affairs (MA, 1984). During the course of a long career in state government in which he served as a key advisor to two New York governors, Howard completed the Program for Senior Executives in State & Local Government at Harvard's JFK School of Government. Howard was awarded the NYS Defense of Liberty Medal for his service during the 9/11 attacks.

While serving in state government, Howard spearheaded efforts to establish a New York State Military Museum in Saratoga Springs, New York, and served as a board member of the NYS Archives Partnership Trust.